A Joyful Noise

Celebrating Simple Gifts

Family Life

Teaching and Retirement

Lessons in Nature

David H. Anderson

snowshoe publications

STAPLES, MINNESOTA

A Joyful Noise
Celebrating Simple Gifts
David H. Anderson

Showshoe Publishing
28728 Snowshoe Trail
Staples, MN 56479

Copyright © 2002 by David H. Anderson

Cover Photo: John Gorton
Layout and Design: Mark Anderson

The main text of this book was set in Garamond typeface.

All rights reserved. No part of this book may be reproduced or transmitted in any form or by any means, electronic or mechanical, including photocopying, recording, or by any information storage and retrieval system without written permission from the author, except for the inclusion of brief quotations in a review.

The purpose of this book is to entertain. The author and Snowshoe Communications shall have neither responsibility nor liability to any person or entity with respect to any loss or damage caused or alleged to be caused, directly or indirectly, by the information contained in this book. Some names have been changed in the interest of privacy.

The Road Not Taken The Poetry of Robert Frost Edward C. Lathem, Editor 1987 Henry Holt and Co., Inc.

The Luckiest Girl © Jodi Lynn Schultz. Used with permission.

Psalm 100:1 quoted from the *Holy Bible*, King James Version.

ISBN:0-9720799-0-4

10   9   8   7   6   5   4   3   2   1

First Printing 2002

Printed and bound in the United States of America

Foreword

Make a joyful noise unto the Lord, all ye lands!

Psalm 100:1

What do you see when you observe nature? I see lessons in life. One of my favorite hiking and rock climbing sites is Banning State Park. I try to picture the turbulent waters caused by melting continental glaciers, and to hear the sounds of rock scraping on rock. How long, I wonder, did it take the sand-burdened waters to deposit enough sediment to form the massive sandstone base, and how long did it take the swirling glacial runoff to erode the kettles that give the river its name? Nature is constantly changing, forming, rearranging. Sometimes loud and violent, sometimes soft and gradual. Sometimes changing so slowly that it appears to be unchanging.

I marvel at the variety of trees in the park. An autumn walk along the Kettle River may find me breathlessly admiring the panorama. I love the tall stately white pines and the majestic red pines. Even the common jack pine adds to the blend. My deepest admiration goes to the trees that grew from seeds deposited in small pockets of thin soil, and have survived by sending roots into crevices and clinging tenaciously to the side of rock walls. I always talk to those trees as I walk by, commending and encouraging them. I might add that I talk to the crow struggling overhead as it flies against the wind, beating its wings and making little progress. Sometimes I congratulate the crow as I congratulate the tree, for persevering. Seldom do I offer the advice that it would be easier to fly the other way. It must know where it needs to go.

Life is about change, and this book is about life. This book is my Joyful Noise.

> DHA
> March 20, 2002

Introduction

I have always found myself surrounded by lessons and illustrations, and this morning was no exception. After picking up a few windblown branches in front of the house, I decided to wander back to the lake. Late August finds me checking for signs of fall and surveying the deer population. The acorns bring deer families through the area almost daily now. The youngsters, never having learned fear, frisk about and munch contentedly, much like children with a new piece of gum. Their mothers use more caution, but in the end the promise of fresh acorns overcomes their concern for unseen dangers, and they quickly devour the new crop and move on. Lawrence Lake is a small lake, too shallow for fishing but providing good habitat for waterfowl and other wildlife. Joyce and I watch the sun rise over the sparkling water as often as we can, and it gives us a sense of belonging to the earth.

As I neared the marshy shoreline, I noticed two perfectly-formed spider web dream catchers. They were anchored to an overhanging branch and the top of a bush, and the sunlight danced off the delicate fibers. Closer inspection revealed a larger web perpendicular to the first two. I started for the house to get my camera, but changed my mind when my practical side asked me what I'd do with another nature picture. I decided to make a mental photograph instead, and studied the architectural miracle with a sense of awe. As I looked around, new webs appeared that I hadn't noticed, and soon it became a game for me to see how many I had walked past without noticing. Delicate but durable, the form and function of the spider web seems amazing to me. A bit like me, I thought, fragile but strong enough to deal with the challenges of parenting and teaching. Now, in a time of increasing vulnerability, I suspect that my own design is also capable of surviving almost any test life has to offer. I find a good deal of comfort and reassurance in that thought.

I've chosen those words from my journal entry of September 7, 1999, to introduce myself and *A Joyful Noise*. This little book is a collection of my thoughts and experiences in the form of short essays, letters, journal entries, and poems. The topics—faith, family, teaching, and retirement—are close to my heart. Much of what I write deals with growing through change. My sincere hope is that you can identify with some of the things I have to say, and that my reflections will encourage you to be still and listen to the voice of Someone I have come to know quite well.

A Joyful Noise

Promise Unfulfilled

It is 6:15 when I first lift my head to peer out the window, acknowledging the fact that I have known for almost half an hour. I'm not going to sleep any more, even though it is a Saturday morning. The predawn color show has begun over the small lake behind our house, and although partly obscured by a thick cover of oak trees, it is promising me things I can't resist. I put on my robe and splash some water on my face, making a half-hearted attempt to bring an independent rooster tail into conformity. Nobody will see me anyway. I scurry from room to room, testing the view from several vantage points. How many times have I arrived early to choose the best seat in the house, I wonder. There is a restlessness about me in the morning, something I used to satisfy with a few miles of running. I wander to the basement, opening windows to let the cool morning air float into the house in preparation for another hot August afternoon. Settling down on the love seat, I select that as a compromise. Filtering through the leaves and limbs of the oak trees, the rich colors fill the horizon and whisper that the best is yet to come. Could I capture this all on film, I ask myself, and then choose to let it be recorded instead in my memory. Waiting gives me the opportunity to say a prayer for my grandchildren, but I lose my thought process after the second one. I'm just not a very disciplined person, I decide. Will I miss anything if I scramble into the kitchen for some cereal, I wonder at 6:25. I fill my bowl with Grape Nuts™ and return to the dining room table, watching the reds fade into golds as I eat. The throaty call of a bittern invites me out to the deck where a chorus of morning sounds accompanies the reality that the sky getting cloudy. I return to the loveseat with a cup of cof-

David H. Anderson

fee, spilling a few drops of hot liquid on my bare leg. No problem, I missed the carpet. Could it be that the sunrise has somehow avoided my awareness? I'm still wondering at 6:35 and I return to the basement, where a new bit of percussion has entered the concert. After watching anxiously to see what might be coming around the corner of the garage, I realize that I'm listening to acorns dropping onto the overturned canoe. A flock of crows pretends to be country singers, and the gray squirrels proclaim the official opening of their day, but by 6:50 it's clear to me that the sunrise spectacular that I got out of bed to observe isn't going to happen. In a moment of deeper awareness, I realize that the promise of the sunrise encouraged me to participate in a morning symphony, and I feel no regret that the substitution was made. Maybe we'll get some rain, I decide. It's getting pretty dry again. What would life be without a promise?

August 28, 1999

Promise Delivered

Yesterday proved to be a lovely late summer day, and I closed it by standing on the deck at midnight viewing the night sky with my wife, Joyce, our son Mark, and his wife Caytie. The moon was slightly past full, and we had to look closely to see that it was beyond its prime. The light from thousands of stars penetrated the darkness separating us, yet it didn't occur to me that we were observing light sent out in the recent past and only arriving now for us to see as we stargaze. Mark grew up right here in central Minnesota, while Caytie was raised in the beautiful Mississippi River bluff areas of east central Iowa. Both are familiar with crystal night skies, and they shared stories of the constellations before we decided that it was indeed time to call it a day.

 The crisp night air let us sleep with blankets, quite a change from the tropical heat wave we'd been experiencing. When the sunrise started whispering to me a little before six o'clock, I decided to watch it from the warmth and coziness of my bed. I peeked out the window every couple minutes to note the unfolding of this new day. The colors were more subtle than yesterday, with just a touch of pink making the blues more pronounced. A higher level of clarity showed me that I had been expecting the actual sunrise popover too early yesterday, and I soon put on my robe to get a better view from the living room. I marveled as I watched the process from first sliver of sun above the trees to its gorgeous reflection on the water. The real thing, it occurred to me, arrived with less splendor and boastfulness than the untrue infatuation of yesterday. Courtship has little to do with the depth and durability of a long term relationship. I say a prayer of gratitude for my lasting marriage as I pour my cup of morning coffee,

David H. Anderson

and I wonder when the others who are sleeping so peacefully think these thoughts.

August 29, 1999

Thoughts on Being a Husband

Sometimes I need to remind myself to "make hay while the sun shines." This morning I did just that, taking a solitary thirty-mile bike ride in the crisp stillness of a September morning. My route took me to the hamlet of Philbrook and on through some beautiful agricultural land to highway 10 south of Motley. Although it's not among the most productive land in rural Minnesota, I enjoy this area. It's peaceful on these tarred country roads, and I seldom have to compete with traffic. Being a list maker, I had planned to begin writing about being a husband this morning. As I pedaled, I reflected upon what wisdom I might share. Riding and dreaming, I startled a young brush wolf that was as surprised by the encounter as I, and watched it lope across an open field. My mind went on hold again and I rode mechanically until I heard an unusual outdoor sound, loud and metallic. I stopped for a better look and rousted a pair of sandhill cranes from their tranquility. As they flew away together, I thought of the comeback the once endangered sandhill cranes have made. There was a beauty to their awkward flight, a beauty perhaps inspired by their willingness to stick together. That's what marriage is all about, I thought.

Joyce and I were married young. She had just graduated from high school and I from college. The next few years were action-packed and exciting. I began my teaching career in the summer of 1966, just one week before our wedding. In late July, I was hospitalized with hepatitis. As Joyce drove to St. Joseph's Medical Center in Brainerd to visit me, she had to stop on the side of the road. She was experiencing some early indications of pregnancy, and since I had been called to report for a physical for induction into the US Army, she prayed that she in fact was pregnant. A long bout with hepatitis disqualified me from military service and kept me from being sent to Viet Nam. Joyce gave birth to our first child on March 21, 1967. Instead of a living in a dorm room, studying for tests, and living a life relatively free from responsibility, Joyce was changing diapers and adjusting to all the demands and compromises married life requires. Two other children followed soon, and by the time Joyce was twenty-two years old, we were the parents of three children. Most young husbands are remarkably insensitive and self-centered, and I'm sure I fit that description. No one receives much training in being a spouse and many of us didn't have the luxury of good role models. Both Joyce and I were committed to making our marriage work. We really never considered that there was an alternative. Our commitment to one another carried us through times when our communication skills were still developing. Things happen and people change, it's true. But if both partners agree that their marriage is a priority and are committed to working through any problems, their odds of success rise tremendously. Commitment, communication, and compromise are essential ingredients of a successful marriage. Couples with all of these traits can usually make "for better or worse, for richer or poorer, through sickness or health, until death" become a reality.

  One of the clichés I frequently use is that being the right partner in marriage is as important as finding the right partner. So what is being a husband all about? Believe it or not, I don't think it's about being the "head of the household." That image is accepted and perpetuated by male-dominated couples. I don't think the husband should dominate any more than I think the wife should be the dominant person. Marriage is about partnership, and partnership involves using your combined skills and talents in the way that works best for you. Partners are equal but not identical. If the wife is the better decision maker, she should use those skills. If the husband is the better cook, that's great. Is keeping the budget more masculine or feminine? Neither, is my answer. Let the better organizer lay out the figures. Both should agree on goals and ways of meeting those goals. Children with two parents should be aware that they in fact have two parents, and parenting responsibilities should be shared.

In the early years of our marriage we were financially challenged and many of our decisions were dictated by monetary limitations. The task of providing financially for five children proved to be more than I could achieve on my salary, and Joyce entered the work force shortly after we adopted Becky. That move made it possible to manage the material needs, but required more cooperation from everyone. Joyce organized her time and ours quite well, and parents and children alike soon learned about shared responsibilities.

It would be nice if we had had enough maturity on our wedding day to view marriage as an opportunity to help our spouse become a better person. How can I help you grow? That attitude could be the basis of a tremendous marriage, but most of us don't think like that. Instead, we look at how our own needs can be met. Shared commitment got us through our early years and gave us the opportunity to mature as individuals. I certainly can't pretend to be a marriage expert, but I can say that Joyce and I have been blessed with a rich and fulfilling marriage. In our early years, I suspect that we were more couple oriented than was necessary. There were times when we felt we hardly existed as individuals. Today I cringe at weddings when the unity candle is lit and then the individual candles are extinguished. I know this is a symbolic gesture, but I don't think it's necessary or wise to give up our individuality. We did that for many years, until we finally realized that each of us needs to be a person first. If I'm not confident as an individual, then what do I have to offer in marriage? When Joyce and I learned to give each other a little space, our coupleness began to grow. We have always felt closest to each other when we're sharing a project. Doing recreational activities together is important, too. For us that meant a conscious effort to identify things we both liked to do. I have accepted the fact that while I enjoy hunting and fishing, these activities will never interest Joyce. It has been a challenge for me to stretch myself to attempt some of the things Joyce enjoys most, like public speaking, but I think that's part of being a husband. Biking, playing in the band, and dancing are activities we enjoy together. Balance seems to be the key, and the older we become the more we realize the importance of that concept.

Sometimes circumstances require us to put our own needs on the back burner, but we shouldn't turn off the stove. Men need to admit that our culture has been unjustly male dominated in the past and to get beyond those antiquated mental patterns. We need to apologize for the misdeeds of our male ancestors and learn to become more sensitive. Many marriages fail because of unrealistic expectations. We have too many hats for our wives to wear—friend, lover, cook, substitute mother, advisor, confidante, counselor, finder of lost items. When anything goes wrong under any of these hats, we sometimes place blame. I'm really only speaking for myself, but I suspect that some of these are common male traits. Now that I'm in my late-fifties and retired, it's time for me to return some of the support that my wife gave me when I was just learning this job of being a husband.

The Story of the Eight Cow Wife

Long ago, in a place where chieftains ruled small tribes, a young man decided to look for a wife. He inspected the crop of available young maidens and had already considered a couple of possibilities when the chieftain's eldest daughter caught his eye. Although she was at best quite ordinary looking, the young man decided to ask her father how much it would cost to make her his bride. The father was a shrewd businessman, and "reluctantly" decided that he could part with his daughter for three cows. Three cows was a steep price, given only occasionally for an unusually desirable maiden, but the young man agreed without hesitation. He then went home to his herd and picked out his eight best cows. You can only imagine the feelings the maiden experienced as she watched the young man deliver this small herd of cows to her father. History has recorded that this man was the happiest husband ever, as his wife spent the rest of her life being an eight cow wife.

This little story is based on a folk tale I heard years ago, but never saw in print. It influenced many of my actions and decisions as a teacher and parent. There are several possible morals of this story. You get what you pay for. What you think you are, you become. Positive strokes get the best results. When you expect the best you get it. I'm sure you can state the lesson in your own terms. For some reason, I can never tell this story without getting teary and emotional. It is such a simple story of wisdom and devotion. Maybe I'm just grateful that I have an eight cow wife.

Parenting Made Easy
And Other Myths

Like most of us, I never read a book on parenting before I became a parent. That's kind of scary. We provide drivers' training, firearm safety, physical education, and music lessons, but we neglect the more important area of training for parenting. Through a combination of trial and error, good friends, and luck, I survived this far as a parent. Now as I watch my adult children parent my grandchildren, I am relieved to see that I must have done some things right. After our marriage, Joyce and I jumped right into parenting. We never even considered waiting to become established financially or as a couple. Rick was born nine months and three days after our wedding. Kristi was born sixteen months later and Jodi two years after that. Being the mother of three at the age of twenty-two had to be a tremendous challenge for Joyce, but she is one who is always ready to accept a new challenge. Only our last two children were planned, Mark because Joyce realized that she'd be only forty years old when Jodi graduated from high school and Becky because we felt called to adopt a child. Perhaps coming from a family of ten children gave me some experience in handling babies. As I look back, I suspect that I was probably almost too casual about it. We parented with the best understanding we had at the time, as had our own parents. It's good that most conscientious parents stay in tune with new information in the area of child development. We were not provided any prenatal parenting classes, and I wasn't invited to watch the birth of a child until Mark, our fourth, was born. Toilet training was accomplished much younger with our first kids, Rick by the time he was eighteen months old. I'm convinced that wearing cloth diapers which became uncomfortable when wet encouraged the children to seek, or at least respond to, potty training. With our first children, I felt that their behavior was a clear reflection on my parenting ability and I had high expectations. The later children had the luxury of more relaxed parenting. Joyce regrets that breast feeding was not encouraged at the time our children were born. It was considered "old-fashioned" at that time. As we have observed our grandchildren's connection with their mothers through breast feeding, it seems pretty obvious that the push for feeding infant formula as a modern innovation was perhaps a bit misguided.

Joyce was first an at-home mom and then a daycare provider until our youngest child was four years old. We sent them off to school one by one and progressed through all the typical "firsts." Before long we were experiencing a string of "lasts." It's hard to know which was more emotional. Because I taught at the elementary school, it was particularly rewarding to share all of the school experiences and activities with my children. Although we had high expectations for behavior, I don't think we ever pushed our children academically. It seemed that there were enough decisions we made for them, and to a large extent school performance level was the decision of each child. The trade-off for the benefits of being at home with the children before they started school was that we were always under some financial pressure. Because I graduated from college with the usual loans to repay, and since we had no time at all to establish our household financially before our children started appearing, we had to be very frugal in our spending and prudent in our money management. There are a few mistakes I look back at with regret, but on the whole our family worked cooperatively and always with the feeling of abundant love. As parents, we moved toward teaching our children to be independent. We offered help as much as we could if it wouldn't prevent growth, but we also recognized that sometimes children have to stand alone to develop into productive, independent, happy, and well-balanced adults. Standing alone means being allowed to fall, and that was sometimes easier said than done. I honestly believe that keeping the goal of independence in mind helped us in our parenting. Little by little, we learned to relinquish control and to encourage responsible decision-making. There is a similarity between hatching eggs and raising children. As we see the little beak break through, we become aware of the struggle going on inside the shell. Sometimes we are tempted to provide assistance. I've done that myself when watching chicks hatch, and I know now that if we help them out, they certainly will not survive as healthy chicks. It is the struggle that completes the muscle development necessary for the chicks to walk, hold their heads up, and live independently. If we don't help, some may not survive the hatching process, but if we do help, they *certainly* will not survive. Sometimes in parenting, the best help we can give is to allow a bit of individual effort and struggle by the child.

In 1991, when Joyce and I were at the "three down and two to go" stage of getting our kids through high school, we went to a session at the school dealing with parenting adolescents. The crowd was small enough to sit around one large table, but the speaker hit us with both barrels anyway. He spoke as if we are in a constant battle with our kids, and that we have to be careful not to let them gain any advantage over us. As I listened, his approach seemed wrong to me. Although we have different viewpoints, different family roles, and different responsibilities than our children, I have always known that we were on the same team. Our big goals are at least similar to theirs. While he talked of the battleground and power struggles, I sketched my own philosophy of parenting on my napkin. Later I realized it applies to teaching as well. This may be oversimplified, but it worked pretty well for me.

1) Believe in them, and let them know that you do.
2) Set high expectations.
3) Accept them back when they don't meet those expectations.
4) Model responsible behavior.
5) Listen (that's *really* listen!).

David H. Anderson

The goal I struggled with the most is the last. I had to learn to listen to what our kids said and what they didn't say. Joyce was much better at listening than I, and between the two of us it got done. The key to listening is being available when your children want to talk. Another insight learned at the University of Life is that it does no good to set high expectations if you don't communicate those expectations. It's not enough to love your children and be proud of them, if they don't know that you love them and are proud of them. Two-way communication is absolutely critical. Although I didn't include this as part of my parenting philosophy at that time, I have learned that you have to lose some battles to win the war. Decide which situations are negotiable and which aren't, and don't make a big battle over an issue with small gains.

I have included the story of Becky's adoption under the heading *Back to Square One.* Another aspect of our parenting involves foster children, and I have summarized some of our foster care experiences in a reflection called *Foster Care: The Unfinished Portrait.* We have discovered that once you become a parent, the job is never finished. You can't resign or retire. Parenting adult children provides an entirely new playing field with a new set of rules. One of the blessings of parenting is the eventual transition to grandparenting. Like parenting, grandparenting is a wonderful experience, but I think I should save that topic for another time.

Saying 'I Love You' Without Words

Some people are just more verbal than others! When I sort through my keepsakes, I find lots of letters and cards from some of my children. Jodi and Rick are quick to tell us how much they love and appreciate us. But there are other ways. Becky has always been one to send flowers and cards. Five-year-old Mark followed me around with his hammer while we built a house from scratch in 1979, and today we share a love of nature. Mark and Caytie accompany me on nature walks whenever possible, and they are just as overcome by the beauty of creation as I. Kristi is my partner in teaching. When Kristi was in high school she and I team taught the fourth grade Sunday School class. As a high school senior she spent a daily two-hour block of time in my sixth grade classroom as a teacher assistant. It was one of my parenting highlights to pass on my wisdom, skills, and experience as a teacher to a student so obviously gifted in the area of teaching. Kristi is a first grade teacher today and I have been a substitute in her classroom. What a rare and priceless opportunity! Rick, Kristi, and Jodi have expressed their appreciation by becoming wonderful parents, exceeding the abilities of their own parents and never mentioning our mistakes.

Before our family began to outgrow the nest, the kids devised creative ways to celebrate special occasions. One of those occasions was a birthday celebration for Joyce and me. Since my birthday is May 12th and Joyce's is May 14th, we sometimes share a celebration. Joyce and I got up early to take a walk to the river before work on one of those "in between days." When we returned, we found the table set with china and crystal on a red tablecloth. The kids served a lovely breakfast and then we got ready for school. They knew how to make special events really memorable, and they knew how to honor their parents.

When our kids were home, Joyce and I were quite involved in church activities and sometimes depended on extra help from the kids. Our older children said "I love you" by caring for the younger. All of them helped in projects such as housecleaning. We sometimes had a cleaning party followed by pizza. One summer weekend when Rick was twenty and Kristi was nineteen, Jodi, Joyce, and I participated in a weekend retreat. Both Rick and Kristi were home from college for the summer, and both were working as many hours as possible to help pay their tuition. They took care of Mark and Becky while we were gone, chauffeuring them to town and seeing that they made it to the Korean day camp, Camp Kimchee in Brainerd. When Joyce, Jodi, and I returned from the retreat, we found the following notes addressed to Mark and Becky. Both were written on sheets from the same notepad, and each illustrated the personality of its writer. Rick's note specified what needed to be done and when it needed to be completed. Being capable of extraordinary amounts of work in a short time, Rick demonstrated his organizational approach in his note.

> *Mark and Becky*
> *Things to get done before 8:00 p.m. Monday when Mom, Dad, and Jodi get home.*
>
> *1. Pick up everything!*
> *Family room*
> *Living room*
> *Bedrooms*
> *Kitchen*
> *2. Do dishes and do after supper cleaning*
> *3. Take cans out to garage in a plastic garbage bag.*

Kristi's note indicated her personality and strengths, as well.

Mark/Becky

*How was Camp Kimchee? I did everything except
your bedrooms and the cans.
Love,
K.*

Rick and Kristi would be surprised to know that I still have those notes in my Bible. Both are loved for their unique gifts. As a father, one of my most precious gifts is the tight, whiskery hug I get from my sons and the tears in Rick's eyes when we say goodbye. Jodi shares her childcare experiences via e-mail almost daily, and Becky has been the special gift of an adopted child. Her story is elsewhere in this book. All of our children have paid us the ultimate compliment of asking our advice, both as kids and adults. Sometimes we hear the words, "I love you," and sometimes we read them in print, but Joyce and I never doubt that we are loved, honored, and respected by our children.

Letters from Dad

One of the most useful tools in my parenting toolbox was the communication I had with my children through letter writing. Sometimes it's easier to get everything in just the right order when we write it down, and it also provides a priceless record of growing relationships. Some of my greatest treasures are letters from my kids, and I'm sure they still have some letters from me. I wrote letters to mark special birthdays, accomplishments, or events. I wrote a letter for every graduation. Times of intense pain or joy, times of victory or defeat, were also marked by letters from Dad. Some of the letters were intended to give advice, and all were meant to express my love and support. I'd like to share a few examples of letters from Dad. This one was written to my oldest son on his sixteenth birthday.

3-21-83

Dear Rick,

Time marches on, and nothing we do can speed it up or slow it down. It seems that a sixteenth birthday is sort of a milestone, and time begins to speed up when you reach sixteen. It also means a driver's license, with the accompanying freedom and responsibility, and changing relationships. As a parent, I've tried to step back and give you more room to grow. I've tried to do less of your thinking for you. I have to let you make certain decisions for yourself, even when they're not the choices I'd make. Being sixteen is also the beginning of a new stage in terms of dating and girlfriends. I've experienced the joys, excitement, disappointment, and heartbreak of being an adolescent. I've been accepted and rejected—I know them both. As your friend and father, I'd like to pass on some advice. I hope that you will remember it and pass it on to your son some day.

Being a man doesn't mean being tough. Gentleness is much stronger. You don't have to prove that you're big by making someone else small. You don't have to make someone look dumb to seem smart. Treat people, especially girls you've chosen to date, with respect. Respect their intelligence, their feelings, and their fears. Be honest and open in all your relationships. Most importantly, respect the dignity of your friend by respecting her body. You will find that some day, if you base your relationship on respect, you will be blessed with the excellent kind of marriage your mother and I share.

Good luck!

Love,
Dad

I wrote this letter to Rick when, as a high school senior, he suffered a heart-breaking loss in the regional wrestling tournament. Although he wasn't blessed with great natural athletic ability, Rick made up for it by working harder and wrestling smarter than most of his opponents. He missed his entire junior year of competition because of a knee injury, so his goal of wrestling in the state tournament depended on his performance his senior year. After a slow start, Rick won ten consecutive matches. He wrestled well through the district tournament, but then became ill just before the regional tournament. Although he was still suffering the effects of a high fever and other flu symptoms, he pinned his first two regional opponents. Then, although he was leading in his third match, Rick was caught in a move and didn't have the strength to escape.

2-24-85

Dear Rick,

It happened too fast! I wasn't expecting you to be pinned after establishing such a good lead. I covered my eyes for just a second, and then watched you walk off the mat in defeat. I wanted to cry for you—it seemed so unfair. You had worked so hard for six years for just one season of varsity wrestling.

This year, after Christmas, things really fell into place. Your discipline and hard work brought you some big victories, and people were beginning to recognize you as one fine wrestler. Then came the district finals and the flu! Today, wrestling strong in spirit only, you lost a match that should have been yours. Your dream had been snuffed out by one quick slap of the mat.

We've been through other defeats together, and I knew you needed to be alone for a while. I knew, too, that I needed to see you before you went onto the mat again. One short hour was all you would have to prepare mentally and physically for the consolation round.

I knew I'd find you there, alone in the locker room, leaning back and staring through eyes that couldn't seem to focus. There was nothing I could say to you at that moment, so I just sat beside you and shared your pain. I touched your knee, hoping that gesture would communicate feelings for which words were inadequate. I read your thoughts as you read mine. We expressed a love that goes beyond verbal limits. Not one word—but you knew my sorrow was only for you, and that the depth of our relationship had nothing to do with athletic accomplishments. I could feel your internal struggle as you wrestled an opponent bigger than any you'd ever meet on a wresting mat. You wanted so badly to make me proud, and the confusing assortment of emotions that churned and agitated in your mind was too heavy to carry alone. My heart was breaking for you as I shared your load in silence. I wanted you to know that you were free to cry, to yell, and to kick—and you knew that without being told. I wanted you to know that sometimes the will alone isn't enough to accomplish a task, and you knew. You knew, too, that I'd forgive and accept you if you chose not to go back onto the mat, but I knew you wouldn't choose that route. So we sat without a *word. I touched your knee again and left you alone on the bench.*

Back in the stands, I shed my tears for you. Our love is the same in victory and defeat—that will never change. But somehow, I'm more proud of you in defeat. It's at times like this that you show your true depth of character, and I get a clear look at this man who is my son.

*Love,
Dad*

P.S. Maybe tomorrow I'll even be thankful for situations such as these, which have helped us to grow so close.

When I asked Kristi if she had any letters that I might include in this "Letters from Dad" section, she sent a packet of cards, notes, and letters. The "Dear Kris" greeting on each note reminded me of her childhood nickname and triggered a flood of memories. One was a note showing a beautiful sunset and reference to Psalm 121:2, 8 on the cover.

My help cometh from the Lord, which made heaven and earth. The Lord shall preserve thy going out and thy coming in from this time forth, and even for evermore.

Inside I wrote:

Dear Kris, You're a champion in the things that really matter. Life is a combination of happiness and tears, but tears don't last!

*Love,
Dad*

Another note included an inspirational message under the heading, *To You, My Child*. Inside that card I wrote:

Kris, I hope I have taught you these things. I'm so pleased to see how many good qualities you already have. Keep growing. You're special and I love you. Happy Valentine's Day!

Love,
Dad

A third note was apparently sent with a rose and included encouragement and a little advice. I commended Kristi for her good decisions, expressed my appreciation for her willingness to help at home without being asked, and told her how proud I was of her. As in all the other notes, I told her how much I love her. The final letter was quite long. It was dated October 17, 1984. It was written at a time when I felt a little distance between us. In the beginning of the letter I explained why I had scolded Kristi for driving in a way that seemed careless to me. I reinforced the need for safe driving habits and for using special caution when driving in bad weather. After apologizing for not being able to help her with her math, I went on to talk of our need for continually working on our communication.

Sometimes I worry that we don't talk enough, but I don't always feel welcome in your world. You're a capable and independent girl, much like your mother, and I'm not always sure that you have time for a slow-moving vehicle like me. My hope is that no matter how old you are, and whether single or married, I'll always be an important person to you. I need feedback that tells me I'm valuable and appreciated, and I need to give you that feedback, too. Our personalities are such that we don't always understand each other, and this makes communication even more critical. I'm glad we're teaching together. That is a good project to share with you. You are a special, talented, and beautiful girl, Kris, and I'll always love you more than you know. I love you!

David H. Anderson

May 22, 1993

Dear Mark,

    This is the morning of your graduation open house, and as I sat down to write this letter the computer sang "Frosty the Snowman" to me. Even though I've heard that greeting every time I type, it always surprises me just a bit and then makes me laugh. That's Mark! The house is all set up for company and the display in the living room includes an album of the little Mark of yesteryear. You were the shadow who followed me with your hammer, or copied me at the sink while I shaved. I was always aware of your admiring eyes, and it gave me a feeling of needing to set a good example in what I said and did. As you grew, I recognized an unusual level of perception and potential that was far beyond the ordinary. I tried to challenge and program your mind with concepts and possibilities. You were only about six years old when I explained percent to you, and you seemed to grasp the idea quite readily. It was hard for me to let you unfold at your own pace, and I know that at times I pushed and prodded more than I should have. I remember especially the time when I realized that piano playing needed to be your own decision and that whether I agreed with your choice or not, it was not my call to make.

    Through the years we grew together, and I learned the necessity of backing off and letting you be yourself. That was a little hard, since I was so often involved in whatever was happening. You may have become a little tired of me as a religion teacher, for example, after I taught your class in third, fourth, fifth, sixth, seventh, and eighth grades. I'm not sure yet that I walked the line carefully enough between being interested in your activities without being nosey. It was many years ago that I learned Mark doesn't like having a parent take his picture, and that sometimes he prefers to do his own thing without having a parent around at all. So, I looked for new things for us to do together. You were a good bow hunting partner, and those hunting seasons still provide lots of *good memories. I hope we can hunt again some day. Then we moved to water skiing, and you took to that so easily and naturally. Now that you're going off to college, it's time to trade the boat for something more suitable for me to use for fishing alone.*

I have been so proud of you so many times. I never missed a time you were on stage, and each time it gave me a good feeling. I cried every time "Matt" came back from being beaten up by the world in The Fantasticks. I watched as my little boy learned lessons which only life could teach him, and from which I as a parent couldn't protect him. That was more than just a play! It was a real tribute to your musical experiences and contributions when both the band and chorus chose you as most valuable member. I couldn't help wanting the whole town to recognize your talent and to be proud with me.

This senior year has been a challenge, as senior years so often are. The selection of a college and the anxiety of finding financial aid caused no small amount of stress. It was hard for you having so many of your closest friends graduate before you. I'm confident now that you will find that same type of close friends at college. You will find yourself in the midst of others who are like you, and you will grow with them. The financial contribution of both you and your parents remains a concern to me, and yet I know that we will make it. It involves a commitment to a cause we both recognize as very important, and I am happy that we are able to help you reach for your dreams, however unclear they may seem to you at times.

In concluding this rambling graduation essay, I want you to know that I am proud of you, that I will always love you, that I hurt when you hurt and that I smile when you smile. As my child, you have always been one of my most precious gifts, and I will support you in your choices and decisions. That doesn't mean, of course, that I will always agree, but I've been a parent long enough to know that this is the time for you to fly high and free. Go for the gold, be the best you can be, and be true to yourself! I hoped we've provided you with both roots and wings. The door to my house and heart will always be open. Congratulations!

I love you and I'll try to wait until you ask for advice before giving any. Have a fun and safe summer.

Love,
Dad

Since Becky was an adopted child, we celebrated both her birthday and the day she joined our family. This letter marks the seventeenth anniversary of her arrival.

November 13, 1994

Dear Becky,

It was seventeen years ago that I walked the floor with you singing "You Light Up My Life." I was too excited to sleep, anyway. You have brought so much joy to my life since then, and I want you to know that you are just as special to me now. Through the years I've learned that sometimes the best way for me to show love is to change the oil, fix a shelf, or hook up a television. Parenting five teens has been educational, and with each one I realized a little more that too much closeness can smother, too much help can prevent growth, and too many questions can be considered snooping. I've developed the role for myself of "on-call dad" so that when I'm asked, I'll respond. When I'm not asked, I try to keep a little distance.

One of the biggest revelations to me has been that I can fail at a few small things and still succeed in the big picture. To make this happen, one needs a good sense of direction. Then a few detours won't be too serious. You have a good sense of direction. You have values, ideals, and the tools you need to be happy in life. That's what success really is, peace and contentment with who we are.

A Joyful Noise

I'm not sure that I ever shared much of my adolescence with you, but the years from my sophomore year in high school through college were genuinely traumatic. We didn't have a counselor at our school, and I wouldn't have dreamed of telling my parents about it, so I went to my basketball coach with the fears that I was "going crazy." He told me about anxiety and that many people deal with the types of problems I was describing. For several years I avoided places and situations that might cause anxiety—crowds, funerals, hospitals, sitting in front of people, speaking in public—and the list could go on and on. More than once in a tense situation I passed out on the floor, and that was terribly embarrassing. What I didn't know then was that I was experiencing severe panic attacks. Long periods of depression sometimes came with my anxiety, and nobody had any idea what I was going through. I survived those years by trusting God with a simple faith that God would hear my daily prayers for health—mental, physical, and spiritual. The solution was never simple, but I survived through faith, prayer, and a goal of becoming a teacher. I had some detours and made some bad choices, but through it all God walked with me. God is with you right now, and part of the plan for our lives included your coming to us on an airplane seventeen years ago. You're going to do just fine. I love you lots and lots!

Love,
Dad

Thoughts on Family Changes

Joyce and I became a family of two when we were married. We didn't consider postponing having children or the possibility that we might be childless. Soon we became a family of three, then four, then five, then six, and seven. We treasured those years of responsibility and activity. Even though we knew that it would happen eventually, we weren't quite ready for the household to become six, and then five, and then four. Some of my feelings toward having our children grow up are captured in this journal entry.

My son became a man and grew too big for his nest. I knew he would; I even wanted him to. Life is so precious and so exciting that to keep him small, a little bird in a cage, would have been to steal his life from him.

But something inside dreaded that time when my special friend would move away. It crept up into my throat and put raindrops in my eyes. It put movies in my mind of all the loving moments, and growing moments, and hurting moments. The calendar became my opponent, and I knew that I couldn't win the contest. A part of my being stayed at the campus as we drove away. The sobbing of his sisters, his mother, his father and brother made a soft chorus in the empty-feeling car.

He came home again, but he wasn't a boy any longer. The love and pride swelled up in my chest when he told us how much we meant to him. Because of us, he said, he was able to live and grow, to reach out and share, to enlarge the boundaries around his being.

David H. Anderson

I talked to him this week, and then I knew that I will always be Dad and he will be my son, my friend, my partner, my gift.

January 11, 1986

The Luckiest Girl

When my daughter Jodi was first married, she had to be pretty creative in her money management—a situation which has changed little over the years, I might add.

The following poem is the result of one of her budget-stretching efforts. Instead of buying a Father's Day gift at the hardware store, she wrote me a collection of poems.

While I would have appreciated a new fishing lure, *The Luckiest Girl* is priceless. This is one of the reasons I feel like the luckiest dad!

The Luckiest Girl

I'm such a fortunate person,
The luckiest girl in the world.
When I was just a child,
I found a man so dear.
He had a sense of humor.
He was thoughtful and sincere.
He built me up and told me
I was beautiful and smart.
He taught me that what matters most
Is what's inside your heart.
I loved him and he loved me.
What wonderful times we had!
Years have passed. I'm grown now.
And I married a man like my dad.

Jodi Lynn Schultz

Foster Care: The Unfinished Portrait

It's a pretty safe bet to say that most teachers have had students they would like to have taken home with them. Some children come to school loaded down with the baggage of family problems. How can Natasha focus on her reading assignment when the police came to her house last night to take her daddy away? How can Aaron concentrate on his math problems when his mommy spent the weekend in an alcoholic stupor? A safe and nurturing home is a critical element for child development. Parents sometimes get caught in a tangle of complicated and undesirable circumstances that make it impossible for them to provide a warm and loving environment. Child-care providers and teachers see children from less than ideal situations almost every day. Knowing when to get involved and how to get involved is seldom very clearly defined.

Several years ago I had a student in my sixth grade class who really tugged at my heartstrings. Both of Cindy's parents were deceased and she was caught in the crumbling marriage of an older sibling. Joyce and I agreed that if Cindy were placed in foster care, we would get licensed and bring her into our home. In time, she was placed in foster care, and we did become licensed. Cindy spent a weekend with us, but ultimately her caseworker chose another home for her. We had to admit that it was a placement more suited to Cindy's needs than our home might have been. It wasn't long, however, and we were called to take in a sixteen-year-old girl until the end of the school year. We established a policy with that initial placement that we never abandoned, and I recommend this for any foster family. Before accepting a foster care placement, we held a family meeting. Any member of our family, child or adult, could say no to a placement. No reason was required or sought, only yes or no. Unless we were in unanimous agreement, we never accepted the placement of a foster child.

The next few years provided some interesting experiences for my family. Sometimes accepting a foster child into our home meant re-arranging the sleeping arrangements of our children. Since the foster child needed a private sleeping space, Rick sometimes gave up his room and moved his bed into the utility room for a period of time. He was completely comfortable with that arrangement, and we felt that our children would never be hurt by sharing or giving. Most of our foster care placements were fairly short term, including some that were just for a weekend. In one case, a girl was placed with us who had gotten into trouble and had very stringent probationary conditions. Although Rachel* needed twenty-four hour supervision, she and Joyce soon developed a fairly warm relationship. Before long Rachel made some poor choices and violated her probation. We went to court with her and listened as the decision was made to place her in a more restrictive form of residence. Her tough façade crumbled as she cried in Joyce's arms and thanked us for trying.

Wendy was a seventeen-year-old who was placed in our home during the summer. She accepted the love of our family and soon became very comfortable with us. Wendy wasn't accustomed to restrictions, however, and sometimes found our rules too strict. She stayed out all night with a boyfriend once, and didn't think it was fair that she should face consequences for that action. At that point she decided she wanted to go back to her mother, and her caseworker facilitated the move quickly. Guess what! Her mother didn't want her back. Wendy drifted in and out of our lives for some time, and proudly sent us a picture of her baby when she became a mother. A couple years later, on Christmas Eve, Wendy called us in desperation. We stopped our holiday activities while Joyce talked with Wendy for nearly an hour. Although Joyce tried to convince Wendy to join us at our house, we never heard from her again. It's a helpless feeling when someone

A Joyful Noise

reaches out for a lifeline and then lets it go. That's a part of the unfinished portrait.

Karen was a sixteen-year old high school student when she joined our family. She was experiencing a great deal of anxiety and had some fairly significant mental health needs. We learned much about ourselves as we participated in family counseling with Karen. In the end, Karen sought the security of blood relatives and moved out of state to be with her biological family. Some time later, Karen called us with thoughts of self-destruction on her mind. Although we tried to offer as much support as we could by phone, she dropped out of our lives and we don't know where she is today. She is also an unfinished portrait.

As our children grew older, we accepted fewer placements. I discovered that sometimes the reality of loving a difficult child is more of a challenge than the desire to do so, and I learned that I have more limitations on accepting others than I sometimes want to admit. Our last foster child was Carrie. Although she came to us before her second birthday, we were her third foster home. Carrie was with us for two years. She was just a little younger than Becky, and they played together constantly. When it became apparent that returning to her biological mother would not be an option, a long-term solution was sought. Relatives in a distant state learned of Carrie's plight and offered to adopt her. The adoptive mother came to our house for ten days to get acquainted with Carrie in her familiar surroundings. That was before the time of child car seat restrictions, so we packed our entire family into our small station wagon and drove for three days. We spent the night in Carrie's new home, and in the morning we prepared to say goodbye. As we got into the car, Carrie wrapped her arms and legs around Joyce and cried, "Mommy, don't leave me!" Leaving Carrie was one of the most difficult things Joyce has ever had to do, and her sobs were mixed with others in the car as we drove quietly away. Carrie's new family soon requested that in Carrie's best interest, we discontinue any contact with her. Each of her birthdays was noted, and each Christmas we put a little "Carrie ornament" on the tree. Becky, Jodi, and Kristi had each formed a very close bond with Carrie, and her absence was always a part of an unfinished portrait.

One evening in June of 1999 we received a phone call from Carrie's older sister Dawn. She explained that when Carrie was adopted, the family had also requested that fourteen-year-old Dawn discontinue any contact with her biological sister. Naturally, that was extremely difficult, and when Carrie turned twenty-one years old, Dawn got in touch with her. "She's here with me now, and she'd like to see you!" You can probably imagine the excitement of the next twenty minutes as we waited for the knock at the door. When the young woman Carrie stepped inside, she threw her arms around Joyce. They hung onto each other and cried. It was a joyful scene, so different from the last time that the little girl Carrie had cried, "Mommy, don't leave me!" The next few days included some very happy times when Becky, Jodi, and Kristi spent time with Carrie and shared their memories. Carrie had a small picture album that we had left with her, and she had vividly clear recollections of our home and family. Becky searched through her albums and made reprints of some of the photos she had of the two as children. We all talked, laughed, and put several more brush strokes on the portrait that though still unfinished, was much more complete than before. Carrie returned to her home in a few days, but we have kept in touch. Some stories do have happy endings!

A Joyful Noise

The Road Not Taken

*Two roads diverged in a yellow wood,
And sorry I could not travel both
And be one traveler, long I stood
And looked down one as far as I could
To where it bent in the undergrowth;*

*Then took the other, as just as fair,
And having perhaps the better claim,
Because it was grassy and wanted wear;
Though as for that the passing there
Had worn them really about the same,*

*And both that morning equally lay
In leaves no step had trodden black.
Oh, I kept the first for another day!
Yet knowing how way leads on to way,
I doubted if I should ever come back.*

*I shall be telling this with a sigh
Somewhere ages and ages hence:
Two roads diverged in a wood, and I —
I took the one less traveled by,
And that has made all the difference.*

Robert Frost

The imagery of Robert Frost is so uncomplicated. Two quiet roads, two almost equally appealing options. Like the narrator of this poem, I always choose the road less traveled. When I was an adolescent I spent summers thinning rutabagas. The crew was transported to the fields in an old bus, and we spent the day crawling on hands and knees up rows that were sometimes a half mile long. Although the kids weren't allowed to talk while working, I soon learned that if I worked faster than the others the foreman would overlook a little conversation. One scorching afternoon I was crawling along with another boy, quite a distance ahead of the others. "What's your goal?" he asked me. It was hardly the situation for a completely honest answer. I was fourteen and nerdy. He was sixteen and cool in a defiant sort of way. It was even rumored that he was known to sneak across the border into Wisconsin to buy beer. I knew that his ridicule would be hard to overcome. Caution won out, and I replied, "The end of this row!" "No, really," he persisted. I took a deep breath and confided, "I'm saving money for college. I want to be a teacher." As I braced myself in preparation for his sarcastic answer, he responded, "Cool!" Choosing to become a teacher was a bit of a stretch for me, and it certainly was the road less taken. That was a moment that I looked back at years hence, and yes, it did make all the difference! Perhaps it was right then that I realized I could stand alone.

Thoughts on Being a Teacher

When I was eleven years old, a missionary visited our church. After he finished his talk, he suggested that we pray each day for people to answer God's call. It was a variation of the "workers in the vineyard" story. My faith in those days was uncomplicated and unsophisticated, and I accepted his challenge to pray daily for guidance to "my true vocation." A new music teacher came to town that year. Mr. Hagen taught both band and chorus, and I soon decided that I wanted to be just like him. Many of my male teachers became role models for me in junior high, and I realized in seventh grade that some day I would become a teacher. I continued to pray daily about my calling until well into college, but God had already decided that a teacher was what I would be. When I enrolled in college in the fall of 1962, I declared elementary education as my major. I studied the bulletin, determined what classes I would need, and began a systematic march through four years of coursework. My program required 192 credits, and I graduated on schedule with exactly 192 credits. Little did I realize how much of the college experience I was missing by completely neglecting the social aspects and relationships, but my intent was to earn my teaching certificate and get on with life. It was fortunate for me that 1966 was a time of teacher shortages, because I had no trouble finding a teaching position. Even when I limited my search to towns between 2,000 and 10,000 in the northern half of Minnesota, I found plenty of openings. I chose Staples, Minnesota, because a new elementary school was under construction. In my first five years, I gained a variety of experiences. I taught third, fourth, fifth, and sixth grades in both a graded and a non-graded elementary school. Innovation was encouraged in our school system, and our administration was quick to support any efforts to be creative. In that environment, I had the opportunity to grow into my role as a teacher.

After five years of teaching I was granted a sabbatical leave to pursue a master's degree in curriculum and instruction. My half-salary contract paid me $265 per month. Joyce and I moved to Greeley, Colorado, with our three pre-school children. We rented an unfurnished house and pinched our pennies even more than we had before. To this day, we think back to that year as one of the building times in our family and marriage.

When we returned to Staples I became a fixture on the sixth grade team. I will avoid the temptation to write too much about my years as a teacher. One of the highlights of my career was being recognized as Staples Teacher of the Year in 1979 and gaining the level of Teacher of Excellence in the search for the Minnesota Teacher of the Year. When Staples consolidated with nearby Motley, sixth grade became part of a middle school arrangement in Motley. Although I was a bit reluctant to leave the familiar surroundings of Staples, the move proved to be a good one both personally and professionally. When I stood to deliver a little talk at my retirement celebration, I shared my feelings about being a teacher. I explained that teaching and being a teacher are quite different from one another. Some teachers choose teaching to be their job, and see it as an occupation. Others choose teaching to use their skills in the classroom and view teaching as a profession. I chose teaching because God called me to be a teacher, and I never doubted that I had answered God's call correctly.

A Little Child Shall Show the Way

Tears streamed down my cheeks as I sat in church, only half listening to the words of the eucharistic prayer. My mind had wandered to an incident in my classroom, a simple act which condensed the Christian message into one precious moment. The boy was obviously a misfit; an observer could tell at a glance. He was overweight and poorly dressed. The other students were tolerant at best, and yet I could understand their reluctance to choose him to be their partner. He was constantly doing annoying things, and all of us had to work to be patient. Philip sometimes asked me to be his partner rather than face the anguish of being left out. Today was one of those times. We were involved in a creative writing activity, inventing silly verses to go along with a taped piano accompaniment. When the lyrics were completed, the students were invited to sing their finished products to the class. Working in small groups, the students found this to be a welcome departure from routine.

Philip and I finished writing rather quickly, and he promptly marched to the front of the room to share the results of our creativity. I started the tape and nodded a cue to begin, but the music got past him before he could start. His eyes must have conveyed an unspoken message, because a classmate jumped up with a smile and said, "I'll help you, Philip!" She stood beside him, sharing his music and carrying the melody. Philip sang along and returned to his seat with a proud expression of success on his face.

Somehow this spontaneous act of a child was preaching a powerful sermon to me, and I wept as I felt the warm and gentle love of Jesus flowing into my body. How fortunate I am, to be taught by my students. Her willing response, "I'll help you, Philip," was a restatement of the biblical theme, "Here I am, Lord. Send me." What a demonstration of Christian faith and love, to guard the dignity of one less fortunate. Thank you, Jaynie, for being God's instrument.

    February 17, 1992

A Teacher's Reward

He was very tall, with a well-trimmed beard and gentle eyes. "Hello, Mr. Anderson," he said to me. "Hello, Jeremy." I'm not always so lucky with names of former students, especially after nearly twenty years. Time has a way of changing eleven year old sixth graders into adults of every size and description. "Were you a classmate of his?"

We had met at the back of the funeral home after the wake for a young man who had died suddenly and violently. "We weren't classmates," Jeremy explained, "but good friends and hunting companions." After exchanging small talk for a few minutes, Jeremy looked at me quite seriously and said, "There's something I've always wanted to tell you. You said something in sixth grade that affected my life; one word."

At this point I was curious, hoping especially that I hadn't made some negative remark that had stayed in his mind for twenty years. "It wasn't your everyday word, and I really liked it. You wrote it on the upper left corner of the chalkboard—"infinity"— and then you turned and explained what it meant. That word presented a new idea to me, and it opened my mind."

Jeremy's eyes were looking away now, almost as though he had moved back in time. "I wasn't a very good student, you know, and my parents were divorced." I listened as Jeremy recalled the painful memories of growing up in a home where adequate food sometimes wasn't available. He shared how his mother had struggled to raise three sons. Occasionally his mother had taken Jeremy to church, where the concept of eternity became an extension of his favorite word.

"I don't know why I'm telling you all this, but I knew

something was missing in my life, and when I became an adult I realized it was God." Without a lot of detail, Jeremy indicated that his life had become richer and more meaningful after he was able to move from his troubled childhood home. "I wasn't dumb, you know. When I got to vocational school my grades were mostly A's. Something else good happened, too. I met my father one day and we enjoyed a father-son relationship for a year and a half before he died. I wish my brothers could have known him."

Our conversation flowed freely and easily as we talked of times when God had been very patient with each of us. Both Jeremy and I had experienced in God a loving protector who carried us through difficult and dangerous situations. We recognized that God had kept each of us alive for a reason, and that some day we would understand God's plan more clearly.

I thanked Jeremy for sharing his story with me. He had given his teacher the ultimate compliment. Something I had said had touched a young heart and helped it grow. What a humbling responsibility to hold the power to build or destroy, knowing that any word I say, good or bad, may influence the future of some boy or girl.

Thank you, Lord, I prayed as I walked to my car. Help me to be positive and gentle with every little soul you place in my care.

Summer, 1992

Surprise Party Surprise

As a concrete sequential learner, I like to develop a plan for the day and then follow that plan as closely as possible. Don't get me wrong; I'm not inflexible. It's just that I seem to teach more effectively if I have a good lesson plan. Experience has taught me, however, that some of the best learning activities are spontaneous and that teachable moments don't present themselves at my convenience. Yes, I have learned a few lessons about the need to be flexible, especially around May 12th.

Students like to plan surprise birthday parties for their teachers, and although it's nice to be honored in that way, surprise parties also present a few scheduling complications. It is usually necessary for the students to enlist the assistance of another teacher to pull the surprise off, and for that reason it isn't always a total surprise. There are only so many creative ways to get the teacher out of the room, and on one's birthday suspicion tends to run higher than usual.

Sixth graders always thought it was funny when I referred to "my surprise party" a week before it happened. I sometimes told students on the first day of school that my birth date was May 12th and that we would plan on having a surprise party that day. There were times when I truly was surprised, and May of 1995 was one of those times. About three days after my birthday I received a large manila envelope in the mail. It was filled with birthday cards obviously made by very small hands and a letter from a former student.

Dear Mr. Anderson,

Hi! I hope you remember me. I'm sure you're more than a

little shocked to hear from me. I have never forgotten your birthday since I was in sixth grade thirteen years ago. (I think you reminded us of the date more than a few times!) I teach first grade in Danville, Illinois. When we were doing our daily calendar, I mentioned that it is my sixth grade teacher's birthday today. They couldn't wait to make you cards! It was their idea and they were so excited. We talked about the fact that it would be a "belated" greeting (a new word for them) since I'd have to send them to Minnesota (which they looked up on the map)."

The writer included some personal information about her family and greetings to other teachers. Then she concluded, "Again, I do hope you enjoy these cards. They are sincere!" That really was a surprise, and a compliment to be remembered by a former student. Needless to say, a class of first graders in Illinois received a thank-you card from a sixth grade teacher in Minnesota.

Big Shoes, Small Feet

We all have those days, when our list exceeds our energy, and our expectations exceed our accomplishments. October 29, 1992, was one of those days for me. Finding myself overwhelmed by the unlimited needs of my students and frustrated by my limited ability to meet those needs, I began this poem. In the beginning I talked of Mr. Anderson, the superhero, the person who doesn't really exist My tentative conclusion included a plea to just let me hide and be myself. I found that ending pretty unsatisfactory, but I didn't know how to improve it. I returned to my empty classroom on June 24, 1996, after a week of travel and visiting. I had traveled to my old home town and had taken time to contemplate who I was in the past and who I was becoming. New grandchildren and old friends, going away and returning home to comfortable surroundings and familiar faces, walking into my empty classroom and looking at the list of projects waiting for my attention all influenced the completion of this reflection. I wrote, "Today I understand myself better than yesterday, and hopefully less than I will tomorrow. I *am* Mr. Anderson." With that new perspective, I returned to this old poem and added the conclusion. It describes a comfortable resolution of uncomfortable issues, and I find it much more satisfactory than the original. Coming to peace with both our limitations and our potential is a step toward maturity.

David H. Anderson

Big Shoes, Small Feet

He's always there, and he's never late.

He helps me with the math I couldn't understand.

He reassures me with a pat on the shoulder, and gives me a look to let me know when I misbehave.

He talks quietly and listens to three students at one time.

He cares about my sick grandpa and he notices my new shoes.

He shows me how to be responsible and how to believe in myself.

When someone needs his attention, he gives it right away.

He tells stories about himself and his family, and he makes me feel safe.

He lets me know that it's okay to make mistakes and that we're never going to be perfect.

He calls on me when he knows I have the answer and he lets me read when it isn't too hard.

When I meet him on the street, he smiles.

Who is this Mr. Anderson?

Sometimes I think he's only an illusion I've tried unsuccessfully to become. Sometimes the immensity of the role makes me want to hide.

Just let me be myself, I plead.

Who is this Mr. Anderson, I ask again?

Today I know. I hid. I retreated.

I sought out my roots, and when I returned I knew.

I am Mr. Anderson. But I am more than that. I am dad. I am ampa and bapa. I am spouse. I am friend. I am child, and I am adult. I am success and I am failure. I am empty, and I am full. I am faithful and I am unfaithful.

Yes, the shoes are big, and my feet are small, but with God as my partner, I will continue to march.

1996

Teacher Talk

Old teachers never die; they just lose control of their pupils! If you look cross-eyed when you use this line, you usually get a laugh. I love to tell teacher stories and share teacher talk with old people. It's fun to watch the sparkle return to the eyes of an older person when you ask about teaching experiences of long ago. I have had several good conversations with former teachers who are residents in the local care center. This is one of my favorite examples.

Shortly before Christmas the confirmation class from our church went on a caroling adventure to the local nursing home. After we had paraded up and down each hall singing "Joy to the World" and "Silent Night," we encouraged the students to spend a few minutes visiting with individual residents. Most sought the safety of small groups and chose the more gregarious old timers. I noticed a woman sitting alone in a wheelchair, and we struck up a lively conversation. She laughed easily and often, as she shared some of her insight into her increasing limitations. When she discovered that I was one of the teachers with the group, she told me that she had been a teacher years ago in Kansas. That opened the door for a new level of "teacher talk," and soon it was time to leave. Before saying goodbye, I asked her how long she had lived in this facility. "Less than a year," she responded. "How about you?"

December 28, 2001

David H. Anderson

Necktie Magic

◈

When asked once by a student why I always wore a necktie to school, I replied, "It reminds me that I'm in school and can't burp whenever I want." That's not so far from the truth! But there was something about getting up and selecting a necktie for the day that transformed me into Mr. Anderson. Since my retirement I have accepted a number of speaking engagements with my wife. The preparation is never complete until I slip into my burgundy shirt and the tie with the subdued images of musical instruments. Suddenly I am professional, competent, and confident. It's an amazing process, when you consider it, how an old man in blue jeans suddenly becomes an old man in a shirt and necktie who thinks he knows something. In this poem, *Necktie Magic*, I attempt to describe the process. The interaction with my grandchild is imaginary, but the magic is not!

Necktie Magic

Do you believe in magic, Grandpa?
I slipped my necktie over my dress shirt and pondered those
    simple words.
Like Clark Kent being transformed by his cape,
I watched the needle rise on my confidence gauge.

Do I believe in magic?
How else could I explain that suddenly I was becoming
once again the teacher I had been for so many years.

Do I believe in magic?
How else could the timid student who had avoided
freshman speech class until his senior year stand before an
    audience
of four hundred and hold them captive with his stories?

Do I believe in magic?
If not, how will I face the burdens of today and the fears of
    tomorrow?
How will I deal with the uncertainty of my own aging and
    mortality?
How else will I bury your grandmother some day?

The small sweet face is tilted toward me waiting for my
    reply
and intrigued by the process of watching the rabbit go
    down the hole and
around the tree.
Without a touch of dishonesty, I nod my head and pass on
    to this child
of my child another of the truths of the universe.
Of course I believe in magic, don't you?

September 13, 2000

A Joyful Noise

A Retirement Tribute

May 28, 1999

Dear Dad,

You have spent your last day as a classroom teacher. The desks sit empty, the students have gone to greet another summer. There is a stillness, a silence in the room—your room. You know you won't be mentoring another group of young people here. You won't guide and mold them and watch them grow. You think you have made the difference you will make. But I know differently.

When you are great at what you do, you continue making a difference. Your influence will not end with your last "day of school." It will reach into the next generation and beyond.

In getting to know more than 30 groups of students and letting them know you, you have changed the world. You may have uncovered for some a fascination of numbers. Some may have discovered a life long love of reading poetry or writing. Still others may have grown to accept and embrace people from other cultures. Some of your students have probably become teachers themselves and are striving to emulate your teaching methods. All of this is to your credit, and I believe there's more.

I think there is a father somewhere who knows the pure ecstasy of kissing his child because Mr. Anderson was a man and a loving dad. I think there is a woman who knows she can climb to the top of the corporate ladder because Mr.

David H. Anderson

Anderson believed in girls and boys. I think there are children who are disciplined with love and not shame because Mr. Anderson showed his students the value of respect. And I think there are grandchildren yet to be born who will hear stories about a sixth grade teacher named Mr. Anderson. They will tell of his sense of humor, his sense of family, and his love of the children he taught.

Today I commend you; my teacher, my hero, my Dad. I love you and thank you for the difference you are making.

Love,
Jodi

Retirement Thoughts

Journal Entry June 7, 1999

"Have you thought about what you're going to do when you retire?" I guess it's really just conversation, but the question arose often enough to become annoying. Of course I've thought about it. After being a teacher for 33 years and knowing the end of my career in the classroom was just around the corner, it was hard to think about anything else. Having received much satisfaction and self-esteem from my career, at one time I wasn't sure I'd take the rule of 90 option. The rule of 90 combines a teacher's experience and age, and when you reach the magic number of 90 you can retire with a reasonable pension, as well as some early retirement incentives from the school district As I approached the age of 56, the magic number for me, I suspected that I probably would opt out of the classroom at that time. Teaching in a middle school is a high energy routine, and I didn't want to stay beyond my effectiveness. With this in mind, Joyce and I scheduled a meeting with a TRA retirement counselor in December of 1998, the year before I would become eligible for the rule of 90. The counselor showed me the figures, and then told me about another program which would pay considerably better, provided that I take my retirement in 1999. It didn't take long to decide that the financially responsible choice was to retire earlier than I had planned. Wow! My head was spinning. I experienced such a range of emotions, and I began to think of myself as a short-timer. I've always wanted to finish like a professional, so I continued to be an active and positive staff member. In January I began sorting my files and throwing away some of my treasured curriculum materials. Leaving a classroom involves much more than cleaning out one's desk! The sorting and throwing process continued to the end of the year as I wrapped up activities and units for the last time. But what about me, the person? What about Joyce? How much income would we need to generate in order to maintain our standard of living? I scoured want ads and pored over the internet, trying to find a new sense of direction. Maybe I was letting my search for a new challenge replace the emptiness I feared would occur when I walked out the door on May 28th. When my son Mark needed help shingling his house, I became very absorbed in the project.

Finally, after working with Mark three weekends and two personal leave days in May, I decided to focus on the feelings of my last week, and experience the process as fully as possible. My body and spirit were fatigued as I plunged into my last week. The Monday morning drive cross country to Motley was a little teary. A deer stepped out onto the road, and I remembered how often God sends me just what I need to feel peace. When I arrived in my room, an eighth grade boy stopped in to thank me for being his teacher. He left me a letter that he had written. Then a couple of seventh grade girls who had been really special to me stopped in to get a copy of a poem, stating that they'd be back. As the day wound down, I discarded some of my things from the cabinet. Putting all my old grade books into a box, I went home a little early. At home, I e-mailed my kids about my feelings, and received a response from Rick telling me that he was teary also, just thinking about my letting go process.

On Tuesday I took my time getting to school. When I walked into my room, I realized that I was late for my last staff meeting. My emotions were on overload. After the meeting I talked with Doug Shequen and Sue Adams, both former students of mine who were now my colleagues. Doug commented that I looked as good as the first time he saw me, as a third grade student in my class at the Lincoln Model School. When I returned to my room, I was met by another seventh grade girl who asked, "Are you retiring? Why?" That question was put to me by a lot of seventh and eighth grade students, and I took it as quite a compliment.

Wednesday was my last day of class, and it went quite smoothly. On Thursday we took the sixth grade students to the state capitol, my 29th such sixth grade trip. The bus ride was just fine, and I returned without a headache. I sure have put on lots of miles with kids in school busses! I know I could teach a little longer, but like Michael Jordan, Wayne Gretzke, and John Elway, I think it's best to go out on top of your game.

Rick called me at 6:30 a.m. on Friday, just to say that he was thinking of me. Then Kristi called at 7:10, and at 7:15 Jodi wished me well. Knowing that my teaching philosophy is almost identical to my parenting philosophy, this helped me believe that I have done good things in the classroom. I decided to wear jeans for cleaning up, but couldn't quite abandon my necktie, a trademark of myself as a teacher. Go with the flow, savor the moment, and put closure to my classroom goals. That became my strategy for the last day. A seventh grade boy stopped in to visit, and a seventh grade girl came in to give me a hug. Becky called me in my classroom, and then sent flowers, from all of the kids. We sat through a long awards program, and I had tears flowing down my cheeks several times. Why am I doing this? What lies ahead? My students gave me a DQ cake and a bike helmet they'd autographed for me, and we continued cleaning and closing down the room. The year ended as I always end it, with an awards circle and some positive comments. We put the chairs in a circle and had one student sit in the middle, on my comfortable teacher's chair. Our focus, I explained, was to be on positive characteristics of each classmate. After each student responded, I presented the student an award I had made reinforcing one or two of that student's positive attributes. The kids were very cooperative and sincere. When they finished, they told me to sit in the middle. One by one, they told me what they saw in me. Mitch started, and got my tears started immediately. Then Jacob talked about an analogy I had used comparing our class to a dog sled. My goal, I had explained, was to get everyone pulling forward. Yes, they had understood, and they remembered! A boy with behavior problems told me I had caused him to assume more responsibility for his own behavior than anyone ever had before. A girl told me I had helped her believe in herself. Some of the students who had been challenging to me told me I was the best teacher they had ever had. They commented on my willingness to listen to them and to accept them. I've never sat in the middle and cried like I did that day, as I thanked them for their comments and complimented them on understanding what I was trying to accomplish with each of them. Then, at 3:10, they stood up and made their final exit. Led by Justin, almost every student gave me a hug before leaving. I couldn't face the final clean-up at that time, so I drove over to Staples and walked into each room I had taught in there. Room 16, my first fifth grade class, the year Rick was born. Room 15, the sixth grade room where I taught for eighteen years. I stepped into the fourth grade room I used in 1970, and then walked out to the portable which had been my homeroom for about five years. Such memories! Such good people!

When I drove into my yard, I saw that my load of sod had arrived. I don't think the timing was an accident. I've always recognized the value of a project. Brad came to help me create a new lawn, and the back yard looked good when the rest of the family began arriving on Saturday afternoon. It was a great weekend. Five of our grandchildren went to church with us. It's such fun to show them off! Some of my siblings and my mother came for a little party on Sunday afternoon. Harald and Pauline brought their camper, and Brad's parents drove down from Crookston. In the evening we had our big retirement party at the country club, which was open to the public. Lots of people came and said nice things. My own kids gave some wonderful tributes. Jodi wrote a beautiful letter which will always be among my treasures. Mark and Caytie stayed to dance, and then it was over! Everyone left early on Monday, and Joyce and I spent a little while putting the house back in order.

On Tuesday I went to school late and wore a visitor's pass. When I finished cleaning my room, I walked out for the last time. Now I truly am a retired teacher, but I don't feel the urgency to find a job. I'm going to experience the summer with a new motto, "I have time!" Recognizing that the future is now, I hope I will be able to use and share my time without any guilt about wasting some of it. Time is not a commodity, it simply exists. I intend to exist in it, letting time move freely around me without trying to control it. I'm going to accept the luxury of early retirement and enjoy it. Will I succeed? Only time will tell, and I have time!

David H. Anderson

Psalm 151

A Cry in the Morning Fog

I can't see clearly Lord, the mist is in the air.
I'm not sure where I am, and I'm afraid.
My wife has gone to work, but I'm not there.

The earthquake team has gone to Turkey.
They are helping bring hope in a time of despair.
I watched them on the news last night, but I'm not there.

I look at the heroes of our world.
Peace keepers, law enforcers, medical personnel.
But I'm not there.

Look closer, I decide.
Who facilitates services on a local level?
The community, the township, the legislative district?
Or maybe to those dedicating their time to a cause
so frivolous as recreation, relaxation, or motocross racing.
But I'm not there.

The teachers have returned to school.
They organize their rooms, arranging desk and chair.
They laugh and complain and get ready,
But I'm not there.

Work within your church, some say.
Bring Christ to the masses, or the masses to Christ.
But I've tried and now my vessel is being swamped by the storm.
Write a book. Share your wisdom and experience.
Motivate and empower others to grow.
But my spirit is withering and my soul is parched.

Just be, I tell myself. This isn't forever.
Let the darkness surround you and close your eyes.
The sunlight will bring new meaning, new hope.
Tomorrow I will be a new someone emerged from the old.
A frog from a tadpole, a butterfly from a cocoon.
Don't cling too tightly to the past, or the future will never come.
Trust much, fear little.
The fog is lifting, and I'm beginning to see again.

August 24, 1999

This was my first official day of retirement.

Doing Retirement

"How's retirement?" I guess that's a pretty natural question. Most people ask just to make conversation, and it reminds me of my senior year in high school. Then the question was, "What are you going to do next year?" Just as I did in 1962, I try to give a polite response to a somewhat tedious question. Many people follow up with, "What do you do with your time?" To this question I try to assure them that I am plenty busy and that boredom is not a problem. Recently I met an acquaintance who told me that he was going to be retiring in three weeks. "How do you do it?" he asked in a voice suggesting apprehension and inviting an answer. Since I had given considerable thought to that very issue, I offered him some sincere advice about "doing retirement."

Before my retirement from the classroom at age fifty-five, I experienced a good deal of concern about the future. I wondered how I would find the self-esteem that I received from relating to my students, colleagues, and parents—many who were themselves former students of mine. I worried a little about financial matters and keeping our budget balanced while planning for the time when Joyce would also become a non-wage earner. The emotional part of letting go of being Mr. Anderson was more than a small factor, particularly since I had always enjoyed my work. I knew there would be a lot of tears as my last class walked out the door. Being somewhat of a writer, I kept a journal of my last weeks in school and events that were particularly significant or touching to me. I haven't really looked back at it often, but I know that some day I will appreciate having it. After nearly three years, I'm becoming pretty accustomed to retirement, I would like to offer some thoughts that might help others who are asking the same question; "How do you do it?"

Part of becoming comfortable with retirement is adjusting to the concept that not all verbs are action verbs. Sometimes just "being retired" is probably better than "doing retirement." Many of us are accustomed to being very busy and have learned that our society considers hard work a virtue. When someone is recognized as a workaholic, it is frequently done with a certain amount of respect for their addiction. For a variety of reasons, work is easier than recreation for many of us to justify. Over the years I have learned that recreation is an essential and valuable component of every life. I also understand that a life based solely on recreation would not be satisfying to me. My advice to myself and others regarding retirement is based on the following four main ideas.

First, *most of us function better with a certain amount of structure* in our lives. Predictable patterns and routines help remove some of the unknowns from our daily existence. I joke that I am a recovering concrete sequential, but I find that my tendency to make lists continues into retirement. It helps keep me organized and allows me to use my time more effectively for work and play. Many of my evenings are scheduled with activities. I play in a band in Brainerd on Monday nights, and in Wadena alternate Tuesdays. Wednesday means men's chorus and confirmation class. Naturally, one can choose to use evenings in a variety of ways, but I like to have some of them scheduled. I get up early each morning and spend time with Joyce before she goes to work. Our morning routine includes a daily devotion and breakfast. Even if your schedule would allow it, I think one is usually better off not to sleep late very often. Everyone will adapt a schedule to individual circumstances or preferences, but I think routine is critical.

My second major struggle has been with *finding -purpose in my retired state.* When my children were small and when I was teaching, this was never a problem. Later, I had to decide who I was if I wasn't Mr. Anderson, and what talents I could share with others. It was helpful for me to let go gradually of my professional self. I did a lot of substitute teaching the first year I was retired and enjoyed the interaction with the students and staff. My second year of retirement found me more selective of substitute teaching assignments, and the third year I had my name removed from the list. Some of my security blankets, such as my briefcase full of good classroom activities, served their purpose during the transition. Any personal needs to teach are now met through confirmation and youth classes and some adult education presentations I share with my wife. I have discovered that I can become Mr. Anderson any time I want simply by putting on a necktie, but that in dealing with kids out of school it's okay for me to be Dave. Finding purpose now means being available for things such as Food Shelf and Habitat for Humanity. This is sort of a delicate balance, because those activities are fairly intermittent. The adjustment to retirement is a process and I'm becoming more comfortable with short term commitments as time goes by. I suspect that every life needs a sense of purpose but that the urgency of finding something to do for others on a daily basis will decrease with age.

Interacting with people on a social basis is critical. This means simply finding companionship. Some people find companionship quite easily and naturally. Being an introvert, I realize that sometimes I need to actively seek ways to initiate some human contact. There are days when my only interaction with another is, "Paper or plastic?" "Paper is fine!" "Thanks. Have a good day." That's not a lot of conversation, but it's better than no contact at all. I schedule part of my day for running errands in town and if I get a chance to visit a little, I recognize that as a good use of my time. Social activities and work projects present opportunities for meaningful interaction, but as time goes by I am beginning to realize that loneliness can sneak up on me. Sometimes I have to create an opportunity to visit with someone. This might mean calling someone over for coffee.

The fourth area may be less comfortable to some retirees than others, but it is very important. After retirement, ***we must be willing to redefine our home responsibilities and roles.*** This applies to all of us, but especially to those who have a spouse who is still in the work force. My focus here is intended more for men who have working wives. It's amazing to me how our society has allowed men to avoid helping with household chores. Even though both partners are employed, the wife almost always finds herself with a completely disproportionate share of the work at home. The only way I can really understand this is to see it as a throwback to caveman days. Men, think about it! Is it fair for your wife to work at a job and then come home to wait on you? I'm going to spell this one out a little more clearly than the others, and you will thank me when you recognize the improvement in your marriage.

1) Get up when your spouse gets up.
2) Make the bed.
3) Have coffee ready before she leaves for work.
4) Wash the dishes.
5) Throw a load of clothes into the washing machine and fold the load that's in the dryer.
6) Have a meal prepared when she arrives from work. If your schedule gets busy, you could alternate on the cooking.
7) Do the dishes or help with the dishes.
8) Clean up any mess you create.

I've gotten pretty good at the first eight items. The most difficult for me to get going on is house cleaning. Joyce and I usually work together on this one. If you have the resources for it, hiring a cleaning person could be a good investment, even if it's only once or twice a month for the deeper cleaning. Naturally, couples work out their own division of responsibility. I do home maintenance and Joyce does most of the purchasing. I buy some of the short term grocery items locally and we shop together to fill the cupboards. She used to do the budget and pay the bills, but now I actually write out the checks and balance the checkbook and we budget together.

Retirement is an adjustment not for just an individual but for a couple as well. If both partners can retire at the same time, it would be a different type of adjustment. Life after both partners are retired is a situation I have not experienced, but am looking forward to with anticipation. Meanwhile, I will address this bit of advice to a man who retires before his wife. It's not fun for a spouse to get up and go to work knowing her partner has another week of Saturdays. By being flexible and willing to adjust, "doing retirement" can be accomplished with a minimum of permanent scars. If we can embrace change while maintaining some of the familiar, we will soon learn that there is life after employment.

A Joyful Noise

Bear One Another's Burdens

Near the end of a quiet afternoon of being home alone, I put aside my book on traditional healings among the Pueblo Indians of the Southwest and started digging through some cookbooks. I had been looking specifically for a recipe for candied carrots when I got sidetracked on some pickled fish recipes. The phone had been pretty quiet all day, and I picked it up on the first ring. "Hello, is this David Anderson?" a quiet feminine voice asked. "Yes," I replied. The caller went on to explain that she is a childcare provider who has done family-based child care and hopes to have a business in her home again. Because the home she and her husband now own is not suitable for child care, however, she is presently working in a center. After a particularly frustrating day last Friday, she said quietly to no one in particular, "I hate my job." Her supervisor heard her comment and was very troubled by it. The supervisor came to work today and informed the caller that her comment had been on her mind all weekend. Not surprisingly, the moment of frustration had passed for the caller and she had moved on in the job she usually enjoys. Her relationship with the supervisor has become very uncomfortable, however, and the caller needed support. She had called me out of desperation. I visited with her, asked a few questions, and gave her some encouragement. We considered a couple of options and possible ways of resolving the situation. I asked her who was troubled by her comment and she replied that it was only the supervisor who was losing sleep. We decided that ownership of a problem belongs only to the person bothered by it, and laughed a little. She thanked me and told me she felt much better. I wished her luck in her job at the center and we hung up. She didn't tell me her name but I think she said she works somewhere about a hundred miles from here. It seems the *Love my Job/Hate my Job* presentation that Joyce and I made had more impact than I would have suspected.

February 27, 2001

Back to Square One

Two steps forward, one step back. Two steps forward, one step back. That's been a pretty consistent pattern of my faith story through the years, but not always! Sometimes it's one step forward, two steps back, or maybe just a step or two backwards with no forward progress. When this happens, I try to apply the same procedure I use when I get a little turned around in the woods. I stop, stay calm, and think things over. It is helpful for me to think of my life as a faith journey and me as a traveler. Experience has taught me that every road has curves and hills. Sometimes I find myself on top of a mountain, while at other times I am deep in a valley. Both can be quite nice. I *expect* to slow down for bumpy spots and to make an occasional wrong turn. A closed road and a detour sign may provide a bit of unexpected adventure. Traveling my faith highway I have learned to enjoy the sights along the way. I have also learned that I need to stop for rest and that I do not enjoy traveling in the dark. Sometimes, in spite of all my efforts, or maybe because of them, I find myself circling the same old block and making no progress at all. What do I do then?

When I find my faith level slipping, enthusiasm for growth declining, or doubts increasing, I go *Back to Square One*. This doesn't mean starting over; it simply means returning to solid rock where I can begin the regrouping process. For me, this foundation experience is a time when God was so close to me that I couldn't possibly ignore or deny the reality of that presence. That event happened for me in 1977, and I'd like to tell the story.

Those old enough to remember the late 1960's and 1970's might recall this as a time of spiritual growth in many churches. An ecumenical neighborhood Bible study movement called *Key*

73 provided an opportunity for people of various denominations to meet, discuss their faith, and pray together. Joyce and I participated in a variety of renewal groups and retreat experiences through those years. We were the parents of four young children in 1977, and we were also a foster family. Although Joyce and I were quite sure that our family was complete, we found ourselves intrigued by thoughts of adoption. Our children were quite comfortable with the idea, and our third child, Jodi, pleaded with us to consider adopting a Korean baby. Gradually we began exploring the possibility, using a good deal of caution. Each door we opened seemed to move us more in the direction of adoption. In a Bible study one morning, Joyce was asked to read Luke 14:13. "Instead, invite the poor, the crippled, the lame, and the blind." As soon as she read this verse, Joyce knew that God was guiding us toward adoption. We investigated more closely, and learned that a great need existed for adoptive homes for moderately handicapped children. In March of 1977 we attended a session with Children's Home Society in St. Paul and returned with an application. The process had officially begun.

My sister and brother-in-law, themselves parents of an adopted Korean daughter, invited us to attend a speech by Fr. John Powell, a well-known writer and advocate within the pro-life movement. I had little interest in attending, since the date, June 18, 1977, was our wedding anniversary and since it meant a three-hundred-mile round trip. In addition to that, I didn't need to be convinced to support the pro-life philosophy, so traveling to Forest Lake for the evening seemed like a waste of time. Joyce and I went reluctantly, but we came out inspired to help in some way. That night we prayed, "What would you have us do, Lord, to help in this cause?" Little did we know that very day, in a hospital half a world away, our one day old daughter was abandoned. She had been born to a very poor woman who was already the mother of four children. In addition, Mi Yun Choi was born with a congenital defect causing her undeveloped right eye to be blind.

We continued our cautious but steady path toward adoption. One evening we asked a group of friends to help us pray to know God's will. Later, the leader of that prayer group took me aside and explained the process of Christian decision making. He recommended scripture, circumstances, and a sense of peace. We already had the scripture, and circumstances continued to lead us. Potential obstacles were removed and official red-tape melted away. Our home study was reduced to one visit when the social worker from Children's Home Society, who just happened to have attended high school with my mother over forty years earlier, decided that he understood our family dynamics after observing us for one day. When we needed fingerprints to meet an unforeseen deadline and prevent a long delay, the sheriff said he could do it for us immediately. Financial arrangements were facilitated by a loan officer who was himself an adopted child and by Christian friends who gave us a significant sum of money.

On August 11th the adoption agency called. The social worker told us about little Mi Yun Choi, but advised us to take our time and not feel obligated to accept this placement. A day or two later the packet with more information and her picture arrived. Joyce and I were planning to attend our annual couples' retreat at King's House Retreat Center that weekend, and I suggested that we listen for an answer at the retreat. Little did I know how clearly the answer would arrive.

The weekend was a prayer-filled and emotional experience. We celebrated the Eucharist both on Saturday and on Sunday. Saturday, as I stood during mass, I heard God talk to me. Now, if you were to tell me this happened to you, I'd be more than a little skeptical. Sure you did! God spoke to you. But God *did* talk to me. I heard words that were clear and distinct, yet without sound. I heard, "You are in my will." It was a powerful moment, and I began to cry, just as I am doing as I type this story twenty-four years later. Those words would have been enough for a lifetime. Those words would have been the one-time occurrence of the parting of the Red Sea, but then God said, "And I am pleased." My knees were weak and I couldn't stop sobbing. As soon as I could, I told several friends about the experience. Each time I retold the story, I cried and so did the listeners. I shared it with the retreat master. Everyone knew that something major had just happened. I floated around in a daze the rest of the afternoon, and on Sunday we again attended a worship service. Can you guess the scripture that was read? "Instead, invite the poor, the crippled, the lame, and the blind." That was another confirmation, just in case we had any doubts of what we were to do. It wasn't until the next Sunday when in our home church we again heard, "Instead, invite the poor, the crippled, the lame, and the blind," that we realized the retreat master had 'accidentally' read the scriptures assigned for the next week.

Less than two months later, on November 13, 1977, we met Rebecca Joy at the airport. Because her days and nights were a little mixed up, I spent most of that night walking the floor with her and singing, "You Light up My Life." Rebecca Joy is now twenty-four years old. She has completed our family. Yes, God talks to us today. Yes, miracles still happen. And yes, whenever I doubt, I go *Back to Square One*.

March 12, 2002

I am the Prodigal Son

Reflections on Two Parables

I am the prodigal son.
I have ignored the richness of relationships and have sought
 happiness in things
with no lasting value. I have engaged in foolishness and
 recklessness.
I have squandered my inheritance, and I am longing for
 my home.
But I am ashamed.

I am the older brother.
Though I have continued to labor in my father's fields, I
 have refused to be a brother to my brother. I have
 neglected to be a son to my father. I have been
 selfish and judgmental.
But I am proud and self-righteous.

I am the father. In my efforts to establish an inheritance for
 my sons,
I have not been available to them. I have failed to listen
 with my heart.
But if I get another chance, I will do better.

I am the rich fool.
I have sought security in things that cannot satisfy.
But in my concern for the future I have forgotten to
 appreciate the present.

David H. Anderson

I am the guest invited to the banquet.
I have hidden behind excuses to inspect my land, to try my oxen, to be with my bride.
I have ignored the opportunity to share the celebration.
But I am filled with regrets and would like to reconsider.

I am the planner of the feast.
I have sought honor in my ability to control people and events.
When my false hospitality was rejected, I avoided disgrace by inviting the destitute.
But I am learning that I am of no more value than the unworthy guest.

I am the unworthy guest. My objections have been brushed aside and I have been welcomed as I am. There is nothing I can do to earn or repay.
But I am humbly grateful.

March 25, 2001

The Titanic: An Allegory

I've been told that when death stares impassively into your face, your entire life moves quickly before your eyes. This may well be true. I'm experiencing a dramatic summary of my own life right now, as I shiver and bob in the icy water. My mind reviews the circumstances to my association with North Star Lines. As a third generation employee, I have never really considered working anywhere else. Accepting the most humble of positions made it possible for me to sign on at a very young age. Shoveling coal into the ravenous furnaces to keep the boilers steaming, I have become quite familiar with the inner workings of the huge vessels. I was thrilled to be assigned to the maiden voyage of this luxury giant, but also a bit uneasy. Something inside me told me that no vessel is infallible, but I seemed the only one who held that opinion. It can't be sunk, was the almost universal belief, and a certain arrogance surrounded the officers and even most of the crew. The passengers were caught up in the magnitude of the ship and the ornateness of its furnishings. Their self-important air of superiority was passed on to their children, and even the very young seemed to share the attitude of smugness. Isn't it a pity that others choose such ordinary vessels for their journey, they seemed to say. It amazed and troubled me that they were more infatuated with their mammoth, elaborately furnished ship than in their destination. I know it's not for me to judge their motives, but they seem to treat ordinary people almost as if we don't exist.

My mind works differently than some, and it didn't take me long to realize that the number of lifeboats was frighteningly inadequate. The engine room was not without flaws, as well, and I soon took to quietly repairing small problems in hopes of pre-

David H. Anderson

venting major malfunctions later. While others marveled at the size of the vessel, I feared that its size would be the very attribute to ultimately cause its demise. Nothing as massive as this ship can be very flexible, and things that can't bend will eventually break. That's pretty simple to me, but somehow people refuse to look objectively when they are convinced they're right.

When the shock of the iceberg came, I tried desperately to keep the salt water out of the engine room. I called out an alarm and directed the frightened second and third class passengers to the deck. It was an impossible task, however, and nothing could save the ship once the damage was done. We could only hope to get as many as possible onto lifeboats. There is nothing more that I can do now as I struggle in the frigid waves. I watch the unsinkable ship tip upright and begin its inevitable plunge to the bottom of the sea. My body is shaking and my arms are fatigued. Is there anything near that will give me support? I need to hold onto something soon.

September 25, 1999

Song of Songs

This poem requires an explanation before you read it. No, I have not been slipping into dangerous flirtations with younger women. When I wrote *Song of Songs*, I was in the process of changing churches. After many years of active involvement with one local congregation, I found it appropriate and necessary to seek a new spiritual home. Could it be that my flirtations with a new church would be nothing more than fantasy?

This poem represents my mental and spiritual anguish with the thought of returning to my old congregation. The young woman represents the new church, and you can hear a voice saying, "She's beautiful, but she's not yours." I must admit that indecision was seldom my companion on my search. Throughout the process, I felt close to God. It is my firm belief that if God is with me, I can't go too far wrong. Enlightened and inspired by a variety of authors, I soon gave myself permission to seek answers in new places. Could this be what Jesus meant when he said, "Follow me?"

David H. Anderson

A Song of Songs, 2000 AD

*I saw her again today, her dark eyes shining and her smile
    warm enough to melt an iceberg.
Certainly she's been around before, but I haven't looked so
    closely.
Resisting such forbidden glances was much easier yesterday,
But today I gaze openly at her loveliness, daring in a way I
    never have before to savor her beauty.
And from somewhere I hear, "The young are for the young!"*

*Her skin is soft and dark. I have dared to touch it lightly.
Certainly not with passion or lust, but enough to feel the
    smoothness.
Just a friendship, I assure myself. I need someone to listen.
Her slim form glides gracefully across the room and I watch
    hopefully,
But the voice says again, "The young are for the young."*

*So full of life, she is, and her energy makes me feel stronger.
Her hair is smooth and long, and it swishes across her face
    when she turns in the breeze.
The tone of her body suggests an ability I have never seen on the
    court or field,
But it reminds me of a time when I could run like the wind,
    and I quickly take another glance.
Now I am beginning to repeat it to myself. "The young are for
    the young."*

*When she sings, her voice is rich and clear. She sings joyfully
 and with confidence.
I try to stand close enough for my own tenor voice, once clear
 and strong, to blend in harmony with hers.
Her hand touches mine and stays long enough to make my
 heart quicken. It was just a touch, I assure myself. But
 I'm surprised at the pounding in my chest.
And before I have time to wonder again, I hear, "The young
 are for the young."*

*It was no mistake, I convince myself. She enjoys being near me.
I am flattered by the thought and suddenly am filled with
 foolish boldness.
Perhaps she would want me to kiss her, and impulsively I do!
The kiss is warm and light, soft and encouraging, and my body
 fills with feelings I had forgotten belonged to me.
She doesn't resist and she doesn't condemn, but she looks gently
 into my eyes
And says, "The young are for the young."*

January 4, 2000

All Are Welcome

The accumulation of snow this weekend was nearly a foot and a half, falling on the deep blanket already existing from other storms. My birdfeeder wore a tall white hat, and stood as a solitary restaurant in front of my kitchen window. Chickadees and some of their small cousins are the regulars here, but a few well dressed blue jays stop in occasionally as well. The jays are somewhat intimidating to the smaller birds, and they sometimes force the regulars to move aside when they come swaggering in for lunch. It's an interesting level of communication and understanding. The chickadees are allowed to stay but are expected to give up the best tables for the fancy meal-crashers. They are treated with a casual indifference, but seem to bounce back quickly without permanent damage to their delicate chickadee self-esteem. I enjoy watching the blue jays, knowing that beneath their bravado probably lies a loving parent, a trusted sentinel, and a loyal friend. This morning I watched a blue jay while I ate my Grape-Nuts® on the warm side of the window. Suddenly a smaller black and white woodpecker cruised in to the feeding station. The blue jay immediately left his breakfast and flew up to a nearby oak branch, where he waited patiently. The chickadees kept busy patrolling the area, while the blue jay fluffed up his warm down jacket and waited his turn. The woodpecker wrapped his feet around the edge of the feeding platform and drove his beak deep into the life sustaining sunflower seeds. He ate greedily, turning his head from side to side and knocking seeds to the ground. This, of course, delighted the gray squirrels who because of the squirrel-guard have to wait under the feeder for their share of the feast. For several minutes the woodpecker gorged himself, and when he finally flew away I almost expected to hear a loud burp. Apparently his ability to fly was not affected by this over-indulgence, and as soon as the table was empty, a different blue jay settled in from just out of my view and ate a few bites. Not until this large and sleek customer was finished did the original fluffy blue jay move in to finish breakfast. The scene occurred as I drank a cup of coffee and read my morning devotion, and I couldn't help but make the comparison of ourselves coming to the banquet table. Many of us are fairly caught up in our own importance, yet when someone more assertive arrives, we step aside. As I ponder this quiet winter scene and wonder which of those birds I am, I realize that in the bigger picture it really doesn't matter. All are invited, and all are welcome to share in the feast. There is no pecking order at God's table, and perhaps some day we will recognize ourselves as just as valuable but no more so than our fellow diners.

February 26, 2001

Lessons from my Neighbors

It wasn't the first time that my sudden appearance has caught the trio off guard and stranded on the road. I regretted the fact that I represented danger to the three-legged doe and her two youngsters. Last week I surprised them as I drove to town, causing them to seek the safety of the woods via the nearest path through the deep snow. In the absence of a convenient escape, the doe plunged into the soft belly-deep snow and with considerable effort bounded away. She stopped at a fallen poplar tree, unable to muster the energy to jump over and hoping that she was far enough off the road to be left alone. Last year's fawns are more than half grown now, and they handled the snow cover with less difficulty than their handicapped mother. I suspect that the doe was injured by a car. Her right front leg is bent back at the knee and is completely useless to her. We have observed her in the neighborhood for two or three years, and each time she has had twin fawns with her. It was about that long ago that a deer ran into the side of my car as I drove home one evening, hardly causing a dent in the Camry but probably inflicting more damage to the deer. Based on my understanding of deer behavior, I suspect that she might have found a place to rest quietly for a number of days, allowing her injuries to heal. Had that been the case, her front leg might have stiffened up in the bent position and healed in that manner. I have admired her from a distance at times and have resolved that she will always move safely past my deer stand.

Today I was returning from my support group meeting at about eight in the morning when I again surprised the deer on the same corner. Mother plunged into the deep snow on the west side of the road and fought her way through until she was about forty yards away. Her youngsters were less willing to take the plunge and sought a good trail. The front one ran south on the edge of the road with its tail down and the back one had its tail up, but neither bounded. Instead, they ran slowly and deliberately. I stayed back to allow them time for their search, and when I finally turned into the driveway they came back toward where they had abandoned their mother. Finally they sought the security of the woods and moved along the best trail they could find until they stood silhouetted against the lake but somewhat sheltered by the leafless growth of hardwood trees. There they waited to rendezvous with their mother. I watched them for a long time, and they stood nearly motionless. As I observed them, I became aware of a pair of gray squirrels scampering easily along the snow crust and chasing each other playfully up and down an oak tree. I'm sure it is reasonable to suspect that I was the only participant in this drama who wondered about the apparent lack of fairness. The deer accepted their lot in life with resignation and patience, while the squirrels enjoyed the blessings of their ability to simply run across the same snow that made life so difficult for the deer. I couldn't help but wonder why some of us have been the recipients of an easier journey while others have been dealt challenge after challenge. My prayer this morning is that I might recognize and appreciate my blessings and also have the courage and patience to accept difficult situations when they arise. As I finish this meditation, the deer remain motionless, confident in the return of their mother and of their ability to survive.

March 16, 2001

New Year's Resolutions: 1961

While sorting through my keepsakes recently, I came upon my New Year's Resolutions for 1961. The document was handwritten on a piece of notebook paper, and I found it both insightful and entertaining. Working "toward my chosen vocation" was high on the list, as was concern for maintaining a positive mental attitude. I suspect that the social activist comments involved more lip-service than action. Over the years I have taken various approaches toward resolutions of this type, and in the year 2002 I resolved to make a written prayer list and to use it daily. I have simplified my approach, moving from general to specific, and from many to few. At times in my life I have been critical of myself in a non-constructive manner. Since my mid-forties, I have learned to accept and appreciate myself for who I am. God made me this way for a reason, and I am at peace with both God and myself. If I can't be my own friend, how can I expect anyone else to a friend to me?

March 21, 2002

David H. Anderson

As this wonderful year of 1961 is already two weeks gone; As it is off to a roaring start; As the last fifty weeks promise to be as interesting as the first two; Let the following be my New Year's Resolutions.

Be it resolved that I, David H. Anderson;

1) While not conforming to society will come and meet society half way and be a new social person.
2) Continue my war against rock n' roll.
3) Strive toward my chosen vocation.
4) Refrain from making a public idiot of myself.
5) Try to make the 'A' honor roll at least once during the year.
6) Don't allow myself to get too stuck on any one girl without serious deliberation, good reason, and mutual agreement.
7) Do my best to get a job out of Askov this summer.
8) Don't allow any of my friends to talk me into joining the counter revolutionary forces in Cuba.
9) Take a new outlook on life.
10) Talk Dad into getting a newer car.
11) Don't get down in the dumps of depression regardless of circumstances.
12) Learn to play the trombone.
13) Do my best to combat Communism.
14) Have one heck of a good time for the next 351 days.

These things being resolved by me on this fourteenth day of January 1961.

On Aging

The old Buick turned over drowsily and sputtered to life, shaking off the cobwebs of another night in the garage. She backed cautiously off the cardboard placed between her front wheels to catch escaping drops of bodily fluids, took a deep breath, and headed for another day in Motley. Yes, the country road is a good route to take. I wondered as I gripped the ancient wheel just how long the old gal would last. Not much to look at anymore, her rear end damaged long ago by a trailer and her sides showing growing patches of rust. The power windows had worked for a while after I put on a new ground wire, but one by one they retired from active service until the only way to get the mail is to open the front door. Night driving shows her out of focus headlights and emphasizes the somewhat urgent request to "service engine soon." How fast are we going? How far have we gone? I guess those aren't very important questions anyway, and a frozen odometer might fool us into thinking she's younger than she really is. Yes, it was nice to have heat again this winter after a year's rest proved to be just what the doctor ordered for a stuck thermostat, and I don't think the clunks and rattles really mean the transmission is going out. Come on, baby, just another year and a half and you can retire.

Is it just coincidence that my old body is so sympathetic toward my car, I wonder as I get ready for bed. Let's see, eye drops, nasal spray, two ibuprofen, ice pack on my shoulder, spray on my foot. Now, brush the remnants of a once proud set of teeth, oh, yes, set the claritin out so I can take one when I get up to pee. Did I forget anything? Maybe I should cut the nail on my crooked pinky so it doesn't dig into my palm and put on some hand lotion to soften the old leather. Are you ready, Honey? Do you have your mouth guard in place so you don't grind your teeth, your pillow between your knees for your back, your wrist braces for your carpal tunnel, the vaseline on your chapped lips? Let's put our glasses right here so we can locate them easily. I'll put the night light on so we can find our way to the bathroom. Is 6:30 okay? The Letterman Show gets annoying, doesn't it? Oh, well, I'm zonked anyway. Yes, Buick, you were quite a beauty in 1984. We don't appreciate our youth until it's gone. Goodnight, Honey...I said, GOODNIGHT!

May 9, 1999

Same Sunrise, Different Window

One of the mixed blessings of retirement is freedom from a rigid daily schedule. In spite of the lack of a driving routine, I still try to begin each day with a time of meditation. Quite often that puts me in a position to observe the sun rise above the lake, bringing light and warmth to a cold and sleepy world. As a connoisseur of sunrises and sunsets, I observe both events more frequently than the average person. This morning I moved from my recliner to the couch to be in a better position to see the slowly unfolding drama. I was a little disappointed at first when the only color was a narrow band of red. Sometimes the entire sky is illuminated with subtle shades of purple, red, pink, and finally golden orange before the sun peeks over the treetops. Then, deciding that a scarcity of color makes the little there is even more significant, I tuned in to the age old ritual with a little more attention. Soon the first rays became a brilliant splash of gold, and I wished for a minute that Joyce could be watching this with me. It was then that I realized she was indeed watching the sunrise from a basement window as she did her morning exercises. It was one of those simple moments of illumination when I began to understand my own narrow perception of life and the Creator of life. How many times have I assumed that my window provided the only view of heaven? God must find my small boxes, labels, and categories a bit confining, and perhaps my moments of insight cause a small outburst of heavenly rejoicing. God and the angels are high-fiving this morning as I share my inspiration with my friends. I am thankful that God is so much bigger than I can imagine and that my limited understanding and awareness do not make God smaller. Yes, my window is only one of an infinite

David H. Anderson

number of observation points. Some day I will rejoice as I enter the gates and experience the magnitude of God's kingdom. Today I can only say, "Forgive me for the times I have tried to reduce God to something my small mind can comprehend and for believing that my path to God is the only path. Amen"

January 7, 2002

Passing the Baton

Ah, the joys of retirement! Last night was the peak of the full moon, and I had been tempted several times during the night to get out of bed and take a walk outside in the near daylight beauty of our winter landscape. Joyce had to leave for work at 7:15 this morning, so I decided to take a pre-daylight stroll. I put on my coat and hat and walked down our road, watching the perfect white circle of moon as morning light crept over the fields. The woods kept their shadows a little longer, but soon even they had to acknowledge the fact that morning was near. I was suddenly inspired to put on my boots and walk down to the lake to observe the sunrise. Usually I watch this event through my living room window, but today I knew I needed a more intimate view. My granddog Trina, an old Westie with fading eyesight and a gimpy hip, followed me to the lake and walked along on the crust of snow. I found a snowmobile track and walked first to the north and then back to the south. The moon was still bright, although as if embarrassed by being caught out after daylight it pulled a cloud across its face and pretended not to be there. Understanding that the prime of one's life is a very temporary condition, I found the moon's reluctance to let go of this perfect night quite easy to forgive. In the east, the sun gave little hints that it would soon arrive, but teased us with subtle color changes. First it was just a tint, and then a glow. We watched as blends of pink changed to pink-orange and then to red-orange as a sliver appeared over the horizon. The ascent to the top of the tree line was so gradual that I wondered if I could really notice the movement. If I looked away for five seconds, the change was apparent. I slowed my cognitive processes until I knew that I was seeing the confident arrival of a heavenly body well aware of its own beauty and of the effect of that beauty on all who observe. Although neither the moon nor the sun acknowledged my presence, I was quite sure they were aware that I was sharing in their age-old ceremony of the changing of the guard. The circle of life continues, and as the old moves away, the new comes into being. I watched for just a few more minutes until the sun left its colored cloak behind and put on a new white garment. Then I knew that daylight had officially arrived and I returned to the house, grateful for the opportunity to spend sixty minutes in a somewhat unorthodox morning meditation, and refreshed by an event which stimulated all of my senses and reinforced my faith that Someone much greater than I is in control.

2001

Thankful to be a Country Boy

It was a simple and straight-forward statement made by one of my sisters as we chatted about the decline of the economy in my rural area. "There's nothing holding you in Staples anymore, is there?" It caught me off guard, and a minute later I realized that she was suggesting that I might move to the Twin Cities. The thought of trading my uncomplicated life style for traffic and congestion made me cringe, and I responded only half in jest, "You mean move to the metro? I'd rather die young." Realizing that I had reacted too strongly, I backed this up with a somewhat unconvincing explanation that it would be hard to leave friends and familiar surroundings. The truth of the matter is that at this time we still are connected to the Central Minnesota area by Joyce's work. While another community may offer some things which Staples lacks, such as more shopping, it would be difficult to replace the unique things I've found here.

I reflected on these benefits this morning as I biked toward Aldrich, then north on the Nimrod road and across on county road 4 to county road 23 into Verndale. I followed highway 10 to Aldrich and then veered north through the agricultural terrain and a cross-country ride back to Staples. The miles ticked away as I pedaled. My heart was feeling such a connection with the fields and the wildflowers, the old barns and the modern farmsteads. It would have been almost impossible for me not to sing as I immersed myself in the landscape. Forty miles. Two hours and fifty-seven minutes of pedaling, and meditating, and daydreaming and praying. Four or five short breaks for a drink and a stretch. It was a glorious morning. The temperature stayed in the high seventies and the wind was mild. The blue sky accented the woods and croplands. How could another setting, particularly an urban setting, compare? As I considered the rewards of life in the country, I also reviewed the opportunities I've experienced in thirty-five years of residence. My career was interesting and fulfilling. When I go anywhere in the area, someone always remembers me as Mr. Anderson. I wouldn't be Mr. Anderson in any other setting, nor could I ever establish that identity in another place. Old friends and familiar faces surround me. When I ride, people wave to me. They don't always recognize me, but that's how country folks are. I love the roads I bike on and the lakes where I fish. My kind of lakes are quiet and primitive, without speedboats, water skiers, jet skiers, or manicured lawns right down to the water's edge. Here I find nature in its most unspoiled condition. The woods where I bow hunt have become a part of me, and I sometimes drive out to the river just to say hello. For thirty years I have belonged to an excellent male chorus and more recently to a concert band. It occurred to me as I sang with my siblings last Christmas that although many are more talented than I, most have never had the opportunity to sing choral works of the great composers. Most have never had the experience of performing before an appreciative audience.

In my frequent visits to the metropolitan area, I have learned to drive fairly well in traffic. Perhaps I could adjust to being ignored by the throngs of people, each seeking a little privacy in the midst of the crowd. But what would I gain? I love the peacefulness of my country home. I enjoy watching nature out my window. The deer flies and mosquitoes are seasonal, as is the snow. My true friends have been loyal through difficult times, and support is all around me. Driving to Brainerd to buy a pair of jeans is nothing new, and is a rather small concession. Although I am alone quiet often, I am seldom lonely. I suspect that being alone in the midst of a million people would be true isolation. I guess I wouldn't have to live here, but I think I'll stay, thank you, at least for now.

August 2, 2001

Reflections on a Sunday Auction

There's an auction here today
The yellow sign proclaims.
A sad tone of finality encloses the message
and in a moment of melancholy a passerby reflects on the
    scene.
Dad's gone now, it says, and Mom can't take care of the
    house alone.
Who'll bid a dollar for his shovel or rake, take your pick of
    the tools.
The old lawnmower must be worth ten, who'll give ten?
A courageous façade, a sunny fall day,
 But an unexpected tear betrays the attempt, and the truth
    is known.
The loveseat where we sat to watch the old black and
    white,
Its worn flowers looking much like the brown leaves cling-
    ing stubbornly
To the red oak trees, afraid to let go and face the inevitable.
Who'll start it at five?
Whole boxes of memories going together, who'll bid a
    couple?
That was all I could see
Even driving slowly to get around the cars of the bidding
    swarm,
Reminding me much of ambulance chasers or gawkers at a
    fire scene,
But with the final curtain closing,

David H. Anderson

> *It was good to reflect on the ritual of the auction and the*
> *   volumes never spoken,*
> *Being only felt in the hearts of the quiet crowd.*
> *Ruthlessly time marches, slow down, slow down!*
> *Goodbye, house, and yard, and tree house and swing.*
> *   Goodbye and thanks.*
> *I'll be ok.*
> *They all treat me well. The kids call now and then.*
> *Goodbye.*

October 16, 1995

Bigger God, Smaller World

Try as I might to see through the eyes of another, I continue to walk through life with tunnel vision. An audience so small as to be embarrassing, certainly too small to be called a crowd, watched a presentation last night at Centennial Auditorium. It was a Mixed Blood Theater performance of *Martin Luther King's Dream*. At the conclusion, the single actor returned to the stage and led a discussion on thinking beyond ourselves. While most moderately open-minded people would like to pursue that objective, it presents a real challenge.

Our perspective is based to some extent on early life experiences. Depending on where one lived during the formative years of childhood, for example, the Civil War would be viewed as "The War to Free the Slaves" or "The Northern Aggression." Without any thought (and probably for that reason) we pass that attitude on to our children. Now, nearly one hundred and fifty years after the fact, history is presented with an old layer of paint we call blame. It became clear to me as I listened to the discussion that until I can accept events of the past without assigning roles called "right" and "wrong" to various players, I will not be capable of thinking in global terms.

Moving beyond my narrow perspective involves acceptance of the views of others. That is easier said than done. In my teaching days I encouraged students to live their beliefs without excluding the possibility of other right answers. It is wrong to make the jump of logic that since I feel that I am right, you are naturally wrong if you disagree with me. Learning to be open-minded is a long process, perhaps involving more than one generation of thinkers. Partly through conscious efforts of their parents, my children have more tolerance of other views than I have yet achieved. In time, my grandchildren might be more tolerant than their parents. If there is any validity to that type of reasoning, then our world should become a more peaceful world over time. Naturally, other factors enter the picture. In the modern world it is increasingly more difficult to avoid people who are different or to live in isolation. Instead, we must learn to deal with issues of diversity.

Does being tolerant of the viewpoint or values of another weaken my own beliefs? I suspect not, and yet I am surrounded with examples of non-acceptance between religions. Topics surrounding faith and perceptions of God seem to be too personal for most of us to consider other possibilities. While it is purely speculation, I believe that God is much bigger than any single viewpoint can theorize or comprehend. Do you remember the story of the six blind persons examining the elephant? One found a leg and proclaimed that an elephant is like a tree trunk. Another found the tail and said it must be more like a rope. Another found an ear, while still another found the trunk. Nobody's perceptions were incorrect, but all were incomplete. Until we grow beyond the mentality of forcing our beliefs onto another, fighting "holy wars" and leading inquisitions to root out heresy, we will not achieve world peace.

Just as religion and science have never been incompatible in my mind, neither are different perceptions or understandings of God. I can be a disciple of Jesus and believe that the gospel message will lead me to heaven without excluding others. I firmly believe that the only limitations God has are limitations humans create in an attempt to understand God. That's why we create rigid definitions of who God is and inflexible views of how God acts. My vehicle of expressing my spirituality works well for me, and I continue to embrace the understandings and practices of my faith as I know them. I also believe that I am examining one part of the elephant, and that my perception is limited. God is bigger than any of us suspect, and until we begin to see beyond our blinders world peace will be elusive. As an individual, I can only begin with myself. At the risk of sounding simplistic or trite, "Let there be peace on earth, and let it begin with me."

March 15, 2002

A Eulogy

When someone asked me recently if I knew the leading cause of death, they seemed a little surprised with my answer. I responded that birth is the leading cause of death. That seems pretty simple. Everyone who is born will die, while anyone who is not born will not die. Perhaps it's more accurate to view birth and death as two big events of life, like book-ends holding volumes between them. I think it's healthy for everyone to reflect occasionally on the fact that death will certainly meet each of us somewhere on our path of life. I wrote this eulogy in 1983 while on an outdoor education experience with sixth grade students. I instructed the kids to find a private little space in the woods and to do some introspective writing. Naturally, I took advantage of the situation to write a little myself.

Eulogy for David Anderson

It might seem strange that a person would want to write his own eulogy, but I know myself quite well and I'm not sure what anyone else would say about me. At this point in my life, I'm of sound body and relatively sound mind, so death seems to be a rather distant unreality. If I don't sound properly somber, understand that I do not particularly fear death, nor am I preoccupied with morbid thoughts.

We were taught as children that the purpose for our existence was to know God, to love God, and to serve God. I have known Him, I have loved Him, and I have served Him at various times and in various ways. I believe that being with God for all eternity is a natural consequence of a life based on the hope of Christ's promises. Having confidence in my Savior has freed me from fear, and it is from this point of reference that I address these thoughts. We are told to "know the truth and it will make us free." Jesus has made me free to live and die in His grace.

I was born on May 12, 1944, the son of Harvey and Angeline Anderson. I was the fourth of ten children and we lived a simple life with very few frills. Joyce and I were married on June 18, 1966. We moved to Staples immediately and began a happy partnership that resulted in Rick, Kristi, Jodi, Mark, and Becky. Joyce was an excellent wife, and we shared a love which was truly made in heaven. Together we experienced the joys and challenges of raising a Christ-centered family. God blessed us continuously and abundantly, and I'm extremely thankful for His blessings.

I was a good teacher. I hope I'm remembered that way. Although life was difficult at times, and seemed to take more endurance than I could muster, it was rich and full. My family was a source of joy and pride to me. I hope that I'm remembered as a loving husband and dedicated and caring parent. As I write this, at age 39, I realize how temporary this stage of my life is. My children are becoming more independent. Soon they will be adults and life will continue.

The most difficult aspect of this project is having to write with no indication of the time or circumstances of my death. One thing I know for sure, if I'm going to die young it better be pretty soon because my youth is being depleted rapidly. Another certainty is this—if I have coped and managed reasonably well, it is because I can see humor in everything. Even at that, I sometimes take life and myself too seriously. I sometimes become negative and critical. That's part of my nature. But I have tried, and with God's help I was successful in many ventures. If I have hurt any of you, I ask your forgiveness. If you have hurt me, I extend my forgiveness. Remember my effort, not my failures. Remember my concern, not my insensitivity. Remember my loyalty, and not my im-

patience. Remember my laughter, not my tears.

Regardless of time, regardless of circumstances, whether you are a family member mourning or an acquaintance reflecting on your own mortality, know this: My Redeemer lives, and now I have seen Him face to face! Thank you for sharing your love on this day.

October 6, 1983

Parting Comments

People have frequently overestimated my ability, and this tendency is probably most evident in my wife and family. I have enjoyed writing since I was a child, and have used writing as a means to organize and express thoughts that would probably be left unsaid. Joyce has encouraged me to write for publication for several years. Instead, I continued to fill notebooks, journals, and the computer hard drive with stories and reflections. Finally I began to assemble some of the articles, and *A Joyful Noise* is the result. I have tried to focus on things that I know the most about—family, faith, teaching, and retirement. My intent was to provide stories that would help you see God in ordinary situations. If I can offer any advice or wisdom, it is to be true to yourself, even if this means taking a road less traveled. A great sense of peace can come from sharing your gifts, talents, and stories. Thank you for letting me share mine.

I owe a debt of gratitude to the following people:

To my wife, Joyce
> Sometimes words are totally inadequate. Joyce is my inspiration, my hero, and my greatest joy.

To my family
> Thank you for allowing me to put all of us in a vulnerable position by sharing personal stories.

To Mark Anderson
> My son Mark handled the design, layout, and production of *A Joyful Noise*. Thanks, Mark! It was a big job.

To John Gorton, D.D.S.
> The photograph on the front cover was taken by my friend John Gorton on a photo tour of New

Hampshire. We chose it because it captures the spirit of *A Joyful Noise*.

To Don Sanda

Don is the English teacher who taught all five of my children about writing, causing no small amount of anxiety at times. Don proofread the manuscript and offered encouragement.

To Mary Jacobs

The Snowshoe Publications/Communications logo was created by Mary Jacobs, a friend and well-known artist from Shell Lake, Wisconsin.

To Mary Sperley

Mary is an old friend and colleague. She proofread the final manuscript.

To Chuck and Jeanne Jorgensen

Chuck and Jeanne, of Glenn Oaks Publishing in Maquoketa, Iowa, broke trail and shared their experiences. They also shared their design and layout specialist. That technician is my son and their son-in-law.

To you, the reader

I'd appreciate hearing your comments. My address is on the following page.

Snowshoe Communications

David retired in 1999 after 33 years of teaching middle and elementary school students. He has a Master of Arts Degree in Elementary Education from the University of Northern Colorado. His wife, Joyce, has extensive experience with facilitating groups and working with adult learners. She has a Certificate of Ministry from the College of St. Benedict, as well as training in communications and public speaking.

David and Joyce have presented workshops at many conferences and conventions throughout the Midwest on topics such as these:

What a Difference You Make!
In It for the Long Haul
I'm Worth It and So are You
Touching Little Lives; Making Big Differences
Love my Job/Hate my Job
Making Lasting Differences in a Changing World
Does Anybody Know? Does Anybody Care?
Foster Care: The Unfinished Portrait
Parenting Made Easy and Other Myths
Parent/Teen Communication—Let's Talk!

Joyce is also trained as a retreat coordinator and will facilitate retreats for teens or adults. The focus of her retreats is being aware of the presence of God in our lives and growing in faith.

David and Joyce accept a limited number of engagements and may be reached at:

David and Joyce Anderson
Snowshoe Communications
28728 Snowshoe Trail
Staples, MN 56479

218-894-1574
jdanders@brainerd.net

Additional copies of *A Joyful Noise* are available for delivery from Snowshoe Publishing. Please complete the form below and enclose payment of $14.95 per book. This amount covers shipping, handling, and any applicable sales tax.

Discount Order Rates

1-2 books	*None*
3-9 books	*10 %*
10+	*20 %*

. . . .

To figure the cost of your order:

1. Number of books _____
2. Number of books x $12.95 _____
3. Your discount, if applicable (see above) _____
4. Subtotal (subtract line 3 from line 2) _____
5. Shipping and Handling costs of $2 per book _____
6. Add lines 4 and 5 for your total _____

Please make out checks to *Snowshoe Publications*. Books will be mailed upon receipt of payment. Please allow two weeks for delivery. *Thank You!*

Snowshoe Publications
28728 Snowshoe Trail
Staples, MN 56479